Essential Skills
in Character Rigging

Essential Skills
in Character Rigging

Nicholas B. Zeman

CRC Press
Taylor & Francis Group
Boca Raton   London   New York

CRC Press is an imprint of the
Taylor & Francis Group, an **informa** business

CRC Press
Taylor & Francis Group
6000 Broken Sound Parkway NW, Suite 300
Boca Raton, FL 33487-2742

© 2016 by Taylor & Francis Group, LLC
CRC Press is an imprint of Taylor & Francis Group, an Informa business

No claim to original U.S. Government works

Printed on acid-free paper
Version Date: 20150827

International Standard Book Number-13: 978-1-4822-3523-4 (Paperback)

Visit the Taylor & Francis Web site at
http://www.taylorandfrancis.com

and the CRC Press Web site at
http://www.crcpress.com

Contents

Author

Nicholas Bernhardt Zeman started his career in 3D graphics at the University of Kentucky, Lexington, Kentucky, where during graduate school he began working in 3D Studio Max for the first time. Determined to make 3D graphics and games his career path, he left Kentucky for San Diego, where he was offered a job at Red Zone Interactive, a then-small company making the NFL Gameday series for Sony Computer Entertainment. He continued working for them as an expert in character rigging, facial rigging, and facial animation after they were purchased by SCEA until the team was disbanded and the NFL Gameday series was canceled after losing rights to EA for the football franchise. After that, he worked briefly as an animator and facial rigger for SCEA's motion capture and cinematic studio, working on SOCOM 3, among other titles. He was quickly hired by Take Two Interactive in San Rafael, where he continued to develop and manage character rigs on the NBA 2K series, All-Pro Football 2K8, MLB 2K9-10, and NHL 2K9. After almost 12 years in character rigging for sports games, he decided to leave the employment of game developers and focus on the academic pursuit of interactive development and became professor at Northern Kentucky University in the Media Informatics Department and began his own digital media technology company, RHZ Development LLC, where he continues to consult and produce functional games through gamification, mobile apps, and mobile games under the studio brand Little Fish Games and RHZ Development.

Introduction

IN 1998, I WAS WORKING AT REDZONE INTERACTIVE, a third-party publisher for Sony Computer Entertainment America. We were working on NFL GameDay for the Playstation 2, which hadn't actually been released yet. With deadlines coming up and a completely unknown landscape for the development technology, we were in a bind. We *knew* that the Playstation 2 could do so much more than the original Playstation, but we had no idea just how it would work or what it could do! Since I was the only person there with significant experience and time working with character animation using the new software, Maya 1.0, I was tasked with figuring out how we set up the character with all these new tools. Hence, the job of "character rigger for games" was born.

Character rigging had been going on for some time in the cinematic world, where software rendering allowed the artist to take advantage of tons of tools and techniques. But this was 1998—games could barely be displayed in 3D, much less process full character rigs. Usually, the tools, even with the fastest machines, were slow and extremely difficult to work with, requiring a lot of switches for preview optimization and then waiting for a long time for the renders to reveal what the end result would really look like. But in a game development environment, you don't have that kind of time. In fact, everything *has* to work in real time, *all* the time, from any camera angle.

The thing about character rigging, even in those early days, is that not a lot of people were interested in doing it. Most of the game artists were... *artists*: sculptors, figure artists, graphic artists, animators, and so on. Very few of them were keen on the technical aspects of 3D animation and characters, so it fell into the laps of the few technical artists who were out there waiting to solve puzzles and create systems within which the aesthetic art could shine (probably because we weren't very good at the other aspects of art). One of the reasons why I took on this task is because (a) I couldn't draw worth a damn and (b) I secretly liked it. Technical art is a lot like solving a puzzle, but with a visual component to that solution.

As I delved into the process of character rigging, I started to peel back the layers of the things that define character rigging. Hierarchies, skeletons, rotations, deformation techniques, constraints, relationships, kinematics, and above all anatomy are all vital to the creation and maintenance of a good character rig. And these things are not easy to understand. Sometimes, you feel like you need a degree in human anatomy, computer science, and mathematics all at the same time! And that's not an unfair assessment. You really can't do character rigging without some degree of knowledge in all three of these areas.

So I, along with a lot of other talented individuals a lot smarter and more motivated than myself, began pioneering the technique of getting real-time character rigs to work in games. Along that road, I learned a lot about all the skills listed earlier, which go into the development of character rigs for animation and deformation. It wasn't an easy road—a lot of the knowledge that I was lacking had to come from outside sources. Basic coding, anatomy, and vector math were a few of the things I had to learn along the way in order to even be able to put together certain parts of a human-based character rig.

Due to the long hours of all the pioneering character riggers, from both cinematic and game development, many new "auto-rigging" solutions are popping up in multiple packages. These auto-rigging solutions seek to take all the repetitive work out of setting up a character for animation, and indeed they are tremendous time-savers in a lot of ordinary circumstances, when you need to animate or edit motion capture. Mixamo, Poser, and HumanIK are some examples of these auto-rigging systems available. The only disadvantage of these methods is in the "staleness" factor, where everything starts to look the same, as well as the limited functionality of the said rigging systems. A real professional rigger generally must create the rig from the ground up in order to work out every individual mechanic necessary for the proper creation of a character.

This book is not everything I know about character rigging, but it's everything you need to know in order to comprehend the multiple basic factors that go into setting up a proper rig for a 3D character model. I have taken 14 years of knowledge in this area and condensed it into the absolute essentials for you to learn and comprehend. After reading this book and doing the exercises contained, you should be able to take any modeled character from any software package and construct a skeleton, bind and edit skin weights, and create a simple controllable rig for an animator to work with. The book relies heavily on Maya-specific tools; however, it is not absolutely tied to the software. Other packages have very similar tools (they have to), although implementation may differ from one to another. But the basics always apply.

I

Rotation

CHAPTER 1

Hierarchies

1.1 WHAT IS A HIERARCHY?

A hierarchy is a transform-based relationship between two or more objects, or transform nodes. One object is known as the "parent," and the other object is known as the "child." Two objects connected to the same parent are known as "siblings." You can have as many objects in a hierarchy as you wish, and parents can have multiple children, but a child object can only have one parent.

Hierarchies are very prominent in computer-based systems, because they are instrumental in categorizing and organizing data. It's also used in something much more commonly understood by the casual computer user—folders and files!

Folders and files are set up in a hierarchical manner, which is to say that you "put" files or folders into other files or folders, and when you move the folder at the top, the rest goes along with it! In this way, you can organize where stuff is and move it or copy it as a unit. Everyone who uses computers understands this system a little bit, or they wouldn't understand how to use the computer (although I've had several friends who just dump everything on their desktop and clutter the hard drive randomly). This is the core concept of "inheritance," which is what the folder analogy stands for. It simply means I can put an object or collection of objects into another object and move them all around from a single collection. Anything I do to the top-level folder gets applied to the rest of the folders and documents inside of it. For instance, if I "copy" a said folder, everything inside of it is also copied. If I "delete" a said folder, everything inside of it is also deleted (Figure 1.1).

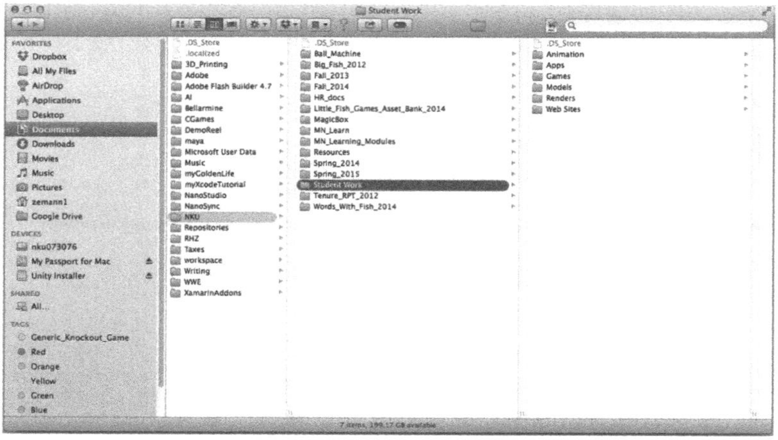

FIGURE 1.1   Windows/Mac folder structure.

1.2 HOW DO YOU MAKE A HIERARCHY IN 3D?

Constructing a hierarchy is actually pretty easy in any 3D graphics program. You select one object, and then another, and choose "parent" or link it in some way. The parent/child relationship is constructed in some manner by choosing the child, then the parent, and establishing the relationship. This is much like making a folder "Parent," in a computer filing system and placing the folder: "Child" inside it. The Child folder is now contained inside of the Parent folder. In much the same way, the child object's transforms in 3D are contained within the parent object's transforms (Figure 1.2).

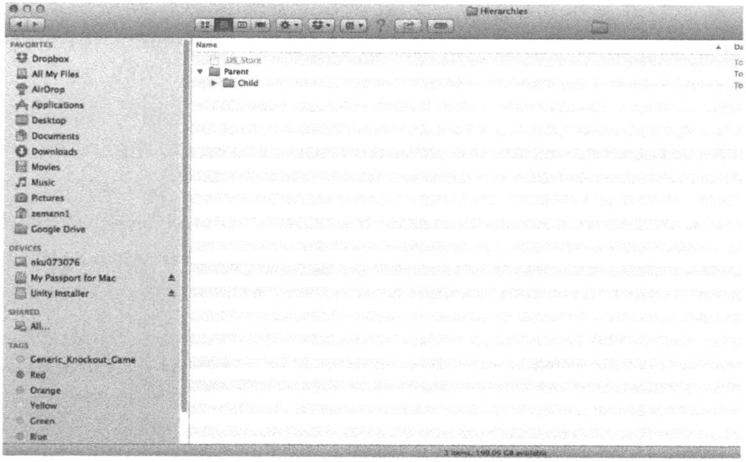

FIGURE 1.2   Parent and Child folders.

In Maya, you can see that when you select one object, that is, the parent of another, both objects are highlighted. This is done to indicate that you have selected an object with a hierarchy, and any objects beneath the selected object will inherit the transforms of the selected object. If you select the child object in this relationship, the parent object will not highlight and you can move it independently.

1.3 WHAT DOES "INHERITING TRANSFORM" MEAN?

1.3.1 How Does the Parent/Child Relationship Affect Global/Local/Object Transforms?

The relationship between parent and child in 3D is a complex one. Let's explore it a little. First, it is the *transform* that is affected by the relationship. This means that if you rotate, translate, or scale the parent object, the child will also be transformed as well. But the "child" object's transforms will not reflect value changes! In Figure 1.3, the cube object named "child" has a translate x value of 5 and the sphere object named "parent" has a translate x of 0; when you move the parent to translate x of 5, the child's transform x value in the channel box as shown in Figure 1.4 remains at 5 even though it moved 5 units to the right with its parent! Why is this?

In order to answer this question, we have to look closely at our old friends, local and global transformation. The values that you are seeing in the channel box in Figures 1.3 and 1.4 are *local* values. This has a special meaning in Maya (and all other 3D packages). *Local* values reflect the position of the

FIGURE 1.3   The sphere is the parent and the cube is the child. The child has a translate x value of 5 and the parent has a translate x value of 0.

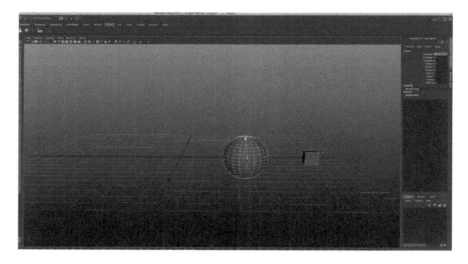

FIGURE 1.4 The parent object sphere has been moved to a position x value of 5, and the child object cube has inherited this transform. The local translate position x of the child object, however, remains at 5.

object *relative to its parent*. This means that its position value in the *x*-axis is still 5, even though its *global* location is actually the world x value of 10. No matter where you move the parent object in space, the child object will still have that value of 5! That value won't change until you move the child object itself. So the local transform value of the child object represents its offset from the *pivot* location (or transform center) of the parent object.

If an object has no parent, it is considered to be a child of "The World," which is basically a fancy way of saying it has no parent and all of its local transforms will be based on the global system. What that really means is that local values and global values will be the same if an object has no parent. Now, every object in a hierarchy can be parented to another, and chains can be formed, where transform inheritance keeps going down the branch—but I'll spare you that headache for now. Let's just get our head around this simple parent/child relationship.

OK, now that we (sort of) get how local and global transforms work with pure values, let us delve into coordinate systems and how they work with hierarchies. Figure 1.5 is the tool box from Maya for translation, which illustrates multiple *options* for translating an object. This is extremely important and misunderstood by many novices. In order to translate the object in question, we must first determine the coordinate system we intend to use. This only becomes really apparent when we *rotate the object*.

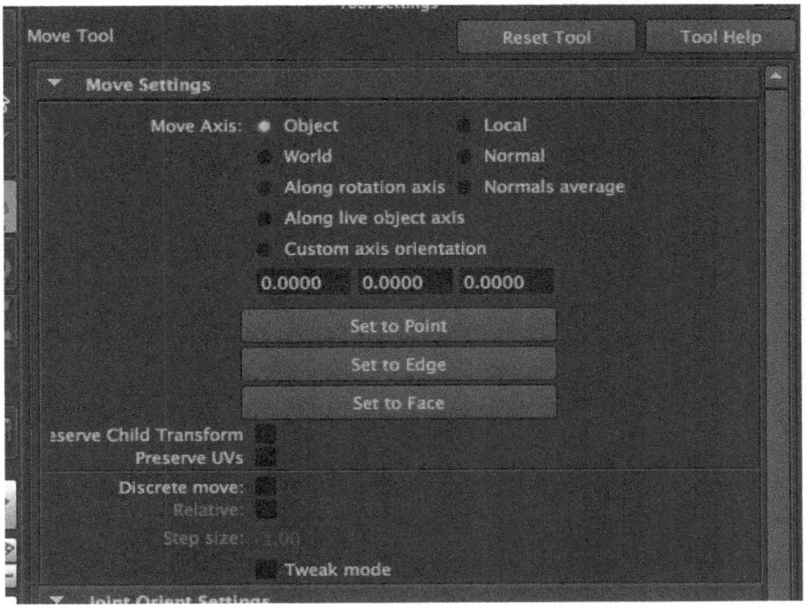

FIGURE 1.5 This lists all the options for translation of an object in differing coordinate systems.

Why? Because when we rotate the object, the alignment of the object and the world become offset and choosing the global, local, or object coordinate system matters a lot.

Let's define these "global, local, and object" coordinate systems first.

Global is the world alignment. Every time you translate an object, it will move along the world axes of x, y, and z. *Local* is based on the object's parent. If the object does not have a parent, global and local will be the same. *Object* coordinate space will move the object in the space of the object itself, despite its parent or the global position.

Now, if you can't quite wrap your head around this, I have a great example that should illustrate the point quite nicely. In Figure 1.6, you can see the parent and child sphere and cube, respectively, from a top orthographic perspective. Notice that the manipulators of the translate tool (the arrow thingies) are oriented so that they align perfectly with the world. This means that if we translate on global, local, or object coordinate systems, the result will be exactly the same.

In Figure 1.7, the parent sphere has been rotated 45° on the Y-axis. Now things start to change. Notice that both the global and the local translations will still be the same, since the sphere has no parent and is considered

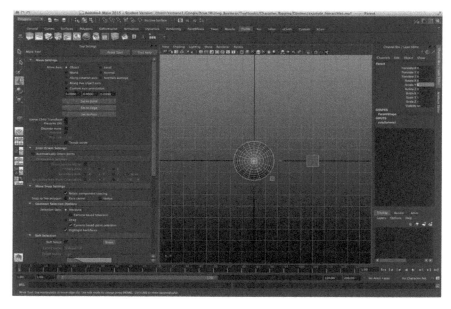

FIGURE 1.6   The object and the world are aligned.

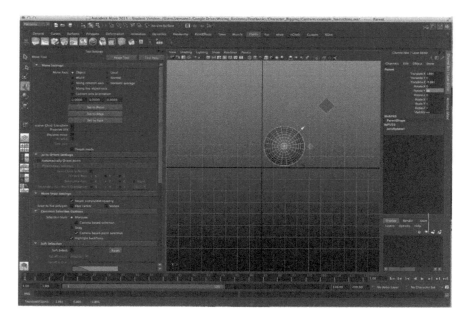

FIGURE 1.7   The parent sphere is now rotated 45° on the Y-axis, which means that its object coordinate system is no longer aligned with the world. See how moving it on the object's X-axis changes the X and Z values in the channel box.

to be parented to the world. But if you choose the object coordinate system and translate it on the X-axis, the axis will not be aligned with the world. Instead it will be aligned with the object! This means that moving it forward on the X-axis will result in a diagonal movement. But it gets even weirder—despite the fact that you can move the sphere forward on the object's diagonal X-axis (taking the child cube with it), the *values* reflected in the channel box are going to change in both the X and Z! Why? Because those are *local* values. You are not really moving the sphere in the object coordinates, you just appear to be. What is really happening is that the sphere is changing its local transform position in the X- and Z-axes. So "object" space is somewhat of an illusion, but a really useful one if you want to have something like a character that always moves forward relative to the way it is facing.

OK, now that we get how all this stuff affects the parent object, let's look at the child object as well. The cube is the child of the sphere, so can you guess what its local coordinate system will look like? Of course, it will be exactly aligned with its parent object in the local coordinate system. In the global coordinate system, the alignment is always the same, for any object at any point in the hierarchy. The cube's object and local coordinate system will also be aligned; however, remember that the *object* coordinate system operates independently of the local system—they are aligned until you change that alignment. Generally speaking, child nodes are transformed relative to their parent, or using the *local* system, but it's not always necessary. One thing to remember in using hierarchies and local coordinate systems is that the child object is now getting its local values from the parent object, which means that the child local transforms are *offsets* from the parent object. If you change the translate and rotate values of the child object to all be zero, then the child will be exactly on top of and aligned with the parent (based on the pivot point).

1.3.2 What Are Hierarchies Used for in 3D Computer Graphics?

Now that you are starting to grasp the way hierarchies control coordinate systems and how we transform objects, we need to understand *why* we use them and what advantages they provide. The thing about these hierarchies is that they mimic the way certain things in the real world work—most importantly our own skeletal structure. They can also represent things such as clockwork, solar systems, or molecular structures, but those things are actually possible to do without hierarchies (although not as quickly).

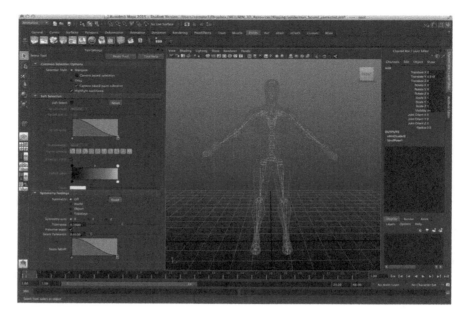

FIGURE 1.8   An example of a hierarchy put to good use as the skeleton of our character.

The one type of hierarchical relationship reflected in the real world that is absolutely dependent on hierarchies to represent them in 3D is the skeletal structure. Skeletons are entirely composed of hierarchical relationships, where one bone is moving both on its own, and in relationship to its parent. Basically hierarchical relationships between joints and bones in your skeleton are the only reason you can get up and walk to the bathroom from your couch instead of blobbing all over the floor like a slug. So if we need to create and develop ways and means for a character model to animate as a human (or alien) might, we are going to need to create hierarchical relationships that mimic the construction of such in a skeleton. In the following chapters, we will learn how to construct skeletal hierarchies and set them up to re-create the mechanics of human movement (Figure 1.8).

CHAPTER 2

3D Rotations

N ow that you have been introduced to the concepts of hierarchies and global/local/object transform space, we need to delve deeply into how rotations are handled in 3D. This is not an easy subject! 3D rotations are extremely complex mathematically and give even the most experienced 3D graphics engineer trouble when working with certain aspects of them.

There are two kinds of rotation calculations used in 3D graphics: *Euler rotations*, and *quaternions*. Euler rotations use three axes of rotation (x, y, and z) in a hierarchical manner (more on this later), while quaternion rotations use four axes of rotation (x, y, z, and w). Euler rotations are far more common in terms of accessibility to the user, and they are far more intuitive in terms of animation and concept. They are, however, less reliable and stable than quaternion.

Quaternions, in contrast, are far more stable and less likely to produce unpredictable results in animation, but are far more difficult to comprehend and set keyframes for. They are, however, very good at blending one 3D rotational state to another, which makes them useful for certain operations and even necessary in things like motion capture interpolation.

But you, as an *artist*, don't have to get into the "mathy" aspects of these rotational calculations. As important as these things *are*, you grasp the fundamental concepts of rotations in 3D in order to move on to the next level and set them up inside of character rigs with joints and skeletons. Quaternions are what most animation engines use under the hood, but few content creation and game development packages actually natively expose this to the user in the interface. *Most* character setup and rigging is done without needing to delve into quaternions. But without getting Euler rotation systems, you will never be able to properly set up, rig, and animate a 3D model.

2.1 WHAT IS A ROTATION?

Interestingly enough, rotations in 3D don't actually "rotate" anything. What actually happens is that the alignment of the object becomes offset from the alignment of the world. Everything that is a child of that transform then changes its position, relative to the parent transform, accordingly. If we are talking about polygonal geometry, in this instance, then the vertices are children of the transform node, and when we rotate the transform node, the vertices all change their absolute position in space while keeping their *relative* positions to one another. So the vertices, when rotating with an object's transform, will retain the same exact same shape, but will appear to be spinning on one of three axes.

This might become clearer in Figure 2.1, where I have a polygon cube with the transform pivot in the center. The *transform* node is the single-pivot object that resides as the parent of the *shape* node, which consists of the vertex information, including their world and local space positions. You can see in Figure 2.2 that I rotate the cube 45° on the Y-axis, and this offsets it from the world alignment 45°. But did the cube transform move

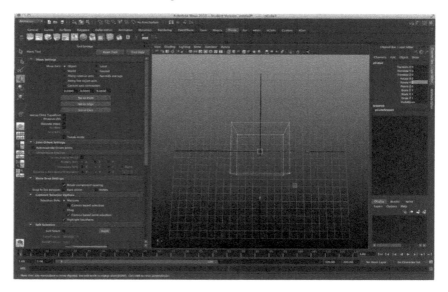

FIGURE 2.1   A polygon cube, with 0 rotation values.

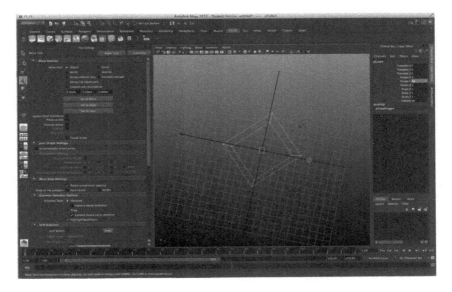

FIGURE 2.2   A polygon cube, rotated 45°. Notice that the vertices have shifted their world positions, but kept their relative positions to one another. This is because they are children of the cube transform node.

in space? Not really. You can see that the vertices that the cube *consists* of moved in the world space while keeping their relative positions from one another. The local positions of the vertices are still all a value of 0; however, they have moved in space.

There are plenty of objects that don't have geometry, such as nulls or empty group nodes. When we rotate those objects, if they don't have any children, then their orientation just offsets from the world, since they are just transform nodes with a point in space designated as their pivot.

2.2 WHAT ARE EULER ROTATIONS?

Euler rotations are, as specified earlier, rotation systems that use hierarchies to determine the 3D rotational state using values for three axes: X, Y, and Z. So to the user observation, they work just like translation/positional data, which also have three values for each point in space. In reality, however, they are much more complex, because you have multiple value possibilities that will all end up as the exact same position in space, but with vastly different ways they can be interpolated in-between. This multiple-possibility solution is what makes Euler rotations occasionally unpredictable or difficult to use, which is something we often refer to as "gimbal lock" (more on this later).

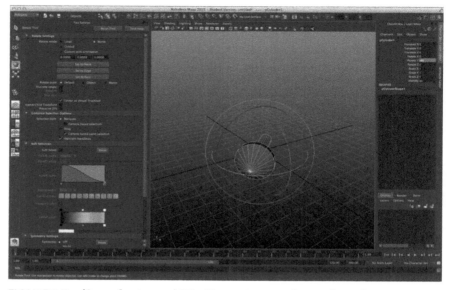

FIGURE 2.3   **(See color insert.)** World rotation coordinates have the same orientation no matter what the rotation channels of x, y, and z are.

Euler angles are hierarchical, which means that each plane of rotation moves independently of its parent axis. This is a hard concept to grasp, but one tool that makes it easier is the rotation tool options in Maya. In Figure 2.3, you can see that I have a polygon arrow with the rotation tool options visible. There are three options: world, local, and gimbal. World is the constant—no matter how you rotate the arrow, the planes of rotation, represented by the circles on the manipulator object in Maya, will remain the same. This is because we are rotating this arrow using the world alignment.

Local rotation coordinates, however, will align all the Euler circles to match the alignment of the object, offset from the parent of the object (which is in this case the world). As you can see in Figure 2.4, the red circle indicating the X-axis of rotation is now aligned with the direction that the arrow is pointing! This is actually an illusion, because if you tried to rotate it on any axis other than the X-axis, it would actually change the values of all three rotation axes! This is because of the way Euler really operates under the hood.

When we switch the rotational coordinate system to gimbal, we see how Euler rotations *really* function. Each hoop or circles representing an axis will rotate independently from its parent hoop, which means that if you rotate the object on the Y-axis alone, such as I did in Figure 2.5, the other two axes will not necessarily follow along with it. This is dependent on *rotation order*, which we will look at in a moment. For now you can see that in Figure 2.5, the X-axis has

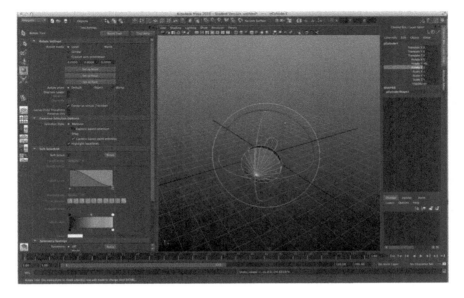

FIGURE 2.4 **(See color insert.)** The local rotation coordinate space aligns all the circles with the direction the arrow is pointing, which is convenient for rotating in specific directions, but is actually an illusion.

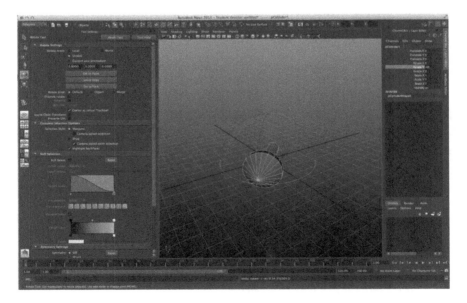

FIGURE 2.5 **(See color insert.)** Using the gimbal rotational coordinate system, the X-axis has changed its alignment to match the direction of the arrow, but the Z has remained the same.

FIGURE 2.6 **(See color insert.)** Gimbal lock occurs when one of these semi-independent circles crosses another axis, such as the X-axis and Z-axis are about to in this image.

rotated to keep itself aligned with the direction the arrow is pointing, but the Z-axis has remained stationary, giving us a very uneven cage. Only the X-axis has shifted its orientation from the world—the Z and Y are still the same!

This can become a real problem when the X-axis plane here crosses the Z-axis plane, as you can see about to happen in Figure 2.6. When this happens, the outcome becomes unpredictable and bizarre things happen to your animations. We call this "gimbal lock" or "gimbal flip" in the animation world, and it's just an inherent limitation to Euler-based rotations.

2.3 WHAT IS ROTATION ORDER?

Rotation order is how the hierarchy is structured for the Euler rotations. It determines which axis is parented to which axis, and which axis rotated independently from the other. Since we went over hierarchies in the last chapter, it should be somewhat easy to grasp how you have one object parented to the other, and that parent is parented to another object. Euler rotations use this simple setup to make it easy to adjust each channel independently, which is far easier to animate but far more complex to interpolate. Rotation order is simply the order in which the axes are rotated. XYZ is the default, which means that the X-axis is at the bottom of the hierarchy, independently

FIGURE 2.7   Rotation order can be changed on any object in the attribute editor; however, changing these values for an object that already has animation data will result in unpredictable results.

rotating, while the Z is at the top of the hierarchy, rotating itself and both the Y and X with it. Although this is hard to illustrate in static images, Lesson #1 will go over it through interactive manipulation. We can always change the rotation order on a per-object basis, which is really convenient to the animator if their animation requires a different ordering to avoid gimbal locking or unwanted interpolations during animation. Changing the rotation order when there are rotation values in the Euler channels can result in unpredictable positions for the object in question—it's best to set this up before any animation has been created (Figure 2.7).

2.4 WHAT ARE QUATERNION ROTATIONS?

Quaternion rotations are a type of 3D rotational calculation that use four directions instead of three. They are not hierarchical, instead use values of 0–1 to indicate the direction of rotation upon the axis. They are extremely hard to animate with, given the extra channel, but they are also extremely stable in interpolation and don't require rotation order. Most 3D packages choose not to expose the quaternion value system to the user for multiple reasons, although Blender, the premiere open-source 3D package, does allow this.

2.5 WHAT ROTATION TYPES DO I USE? WHY HAVE TWO TYPES OF ROTATIONS?

Most of the time the animator can do just fine with Euler rotations, and indeed they are set up to be simple and intuitive for that purpose. Simple rotations on one or two planes only will really not benefit from quaternions at all, since the gimbal locking problem can be avoided altogether. The place where quaternions are vastly preferred to Euler's are where complex blending between one rotational state and another is constantly necessary, such as a shoulder socket or especially camera setups in real-time game environments, where the states must be constantly blended from one to another. In compiled, or rendered, animation sequences, most packages have some sort of "quaternion filter" to fix problem areas of rotational animation data, and the user can avoid ever mucking around with quaternions. Most of the *real* calculations, however, in 3D packages and games are performed in quaternions to be stable enough to handle constant user input data.

You, as an aspiring or current artist, will not necessarily need to know how to set up quaternions, but the fact that they are there and available (in some capacity) can be very useful in those areas and specific instances when you need them, or when Euler rotations simply don't work.

CHAPTER 3

Joints and Joint Orient

3.1 WHAT IS A JOINT?

In character rigging and setup, you will hear the term "joint" or "bone" often. As far as the terminology goes, they are essentially one and the same, the difference being the various software packages and how they like to label them. Since we are using Maya primarily for this book, we will use their terminology, which is "joint."

A joint is a transform node, and like any transform node it has a particular point in space where it is located. Each joint has a World position coordinate. But joints differ from transform nodes in that they are a special type of object and have extra properties that are used when constructing "skeletons," which are hierarchical construction of multiple joints that are used to define character motion using rotations and translations (and sometimes even scale). These special properties are there in order to assist the rigger and animator in constructing rigs that conform to the basic mechanics of movement, which are called "kinematics." Figure 3.1 illustrates what a single joint looks like in Maya, which is simply three hoops together that indicate the direction of the "joint orient" (which we'll talk about in a moment). Figure 3.2 illustrates what joints look like when parented to one another, which appears like a pyramidal structure, with the large end of the pyramid beginning at the parent and the small end terminating at the child.

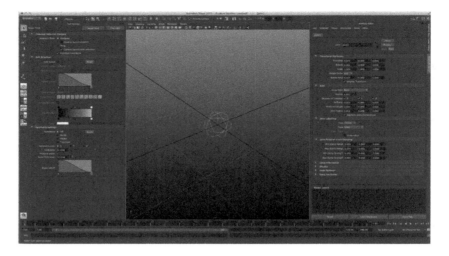

FIGURE 3.1   The joint, as drawn by Maya. Joints do not get rendered in software, but they show up in your interface as three circles, representing their orientation (not their rotation).

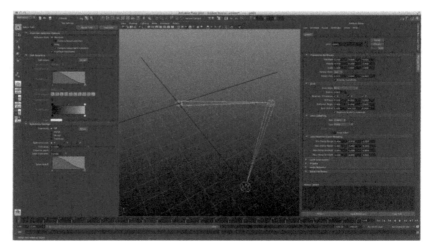

FIGURE 3.2   A series of joints, parented to one another, will display with pyramidal lines, the smaller end terminating at the child node.

3.2 WHAT PROPERTIES DO JOINTS HAVE THAT OTHER TYPES OF TRANSFORMS DON'T?

A joint, being a special type of transform node, has several extra properties that are used in the proper construction of skeletons and character rigs. In Figure 3.3, you can see the extra attributes that are part of the Joint

FIGURE 3.3   All of the unique Joint attributes in the Attribute Editor.

object type in Maya. All of them have some use to us in rigging, however the *most* important aspect of the Joint in this list is "Joint Orient" (so we'll save that one for last).

"Draw style" is simply that; it just determines how you want the joints and skeleton to be drawn in your viewport. In 14 years of character rigging I have never had any reason to use anything but "Bone," which is what we will be using; however, it *is* possible to use other options. But this only changes the way it looks in the viewport. "Radius" is the spherical radius of the joint, which once again only affects the way it looks in the 3D viewport. If you want, you can have different joints of different radii, for aiding your visual model of the skeletal hierarchy, but once again I have always found it to be best to keep them all congruent (which is what we'll be doing).

"Stiffness" is used in "inverse kinematic" calculations. We will revisit this in the next Chapter, which deals with kinematics. It essentially tells the joint to be more or less likely to rotate during inverse kinematic solutions. "Preferred Angle" is also an attribute used in inverse kinematics, which tells each joint the way it "prefers" to move when the solution is calculated.

"Segment Scale Compensate" is a feature that when enabled, makes sure that while scaling a joint nonuniformly in a hierarchy it will not scale the child joint as well. This is important to be set on when scaling joint hierarchies, so that it doesn't create odd deformations in your character. Joint scaling, for the most part, is a very special case and we try to never scale any joint in a hierarchy unless there is a specific reason to do so. A good example of this is the bone scaling that occurs in all sports games, where a single player model is used to define each player on the field or court, but various values for the bone scales can be offset in order to produce taller, fatter, or thinner appearing models. Most of this is handled, at least in my experience, on the engineering end and has little to do with the rigger. However, character rigs that need to be "stretchy" often make use of bone scaling, and there is an entire methodology for creating stretchy joints in order to simulate muscles in advanced character deformation rigs. This, however, is fairly advanced and beyond the scope of this book.

3.3 WHAT IS A JOINT ORIENT?

Now, finally, with that other stuff out of the way, we can talk about "Joint Orient!" I'm sure you are on the edge of your seat. Joint Orient is a difficult concept to get at first, so we're going to spend some time discussing it. Essentially what joint orient does is create a rotational offset from the Euler rotation values. What does that mean? That means that the joint can be pointed in any direction we want, but the Euler rotation values will still be zero. So we can begin a rotation from any joint with a zero, but have it rotate in any configuration relative to the World axis or to its parent. I know this is confusing at first, but as you work with joints, hierarchies, and 3D rotations, you will start to see why this is so important.

In Figure 3.4, you can see a hierarchical chain of several joints, which are perfectly aligned with the World axis. The rotational axes have been displayed for each of these joints to make it easier to get the fundamental

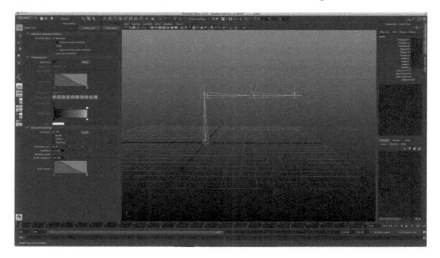

FIGURE 3.4 Several joints in a chain, all of them aligned with the World Axis. Notice the Joint Orients are all exposed in the Channel Box, but both Euler rotational values as well as Joint Orients are set to values of zero.

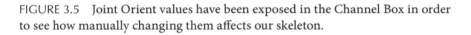

FIGURE 3.5 Joint Orient values have been exposed in the Channel Box in order to see how manually changing them affects our skeleton.

concept of Joint Orient, and the Joint Orient values have been exposed in the Channel Box so that we can edit them manually, as you see in Figure 3.5.

Now, if I change the Joint Orient Z value of my root node to 25, you can see in Figure 3.6 that the entire hierarchy tilts itself 25° backward in the Z-axis! But the Euler rotation values remain at zero. What does this mean? If you remember the lesson from Chapter 2, it means that when I rotate this joint on the Y-axis, it will no longer rotate that axis aligned with the World, but around its center aligned with the 25° offset that comes from the Joint Orient. Figure 3.7 shows what happens when you rotate the joint around its Euler Y-axis.

Now, this doesn't seem all that useful to us at the moment, but I'm going to show you an example of *why* this Joint Orient matters so much. Let's now take our skeletal arm, and change the initial layout of the joint positions in a manner that *aren't* aligned with the World axis directions. Often times, when creating a skeleton for a character, we cannot have every joint aligned with a cardinal world axis. If this is the case, then the joints must be *oriented* to one another, especially in order to generate what we call a "spindle" axis. A spindle axis is where the joint must rotate perfectly around its own axis, while all the child joints in the hierarchy

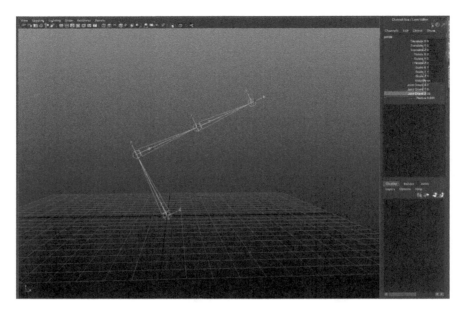

FIGURE 3.6 The joint chain is tilted back, but the Euler XYZ rotation values are still zero! This is because the Joint Orient Z is set to 25.

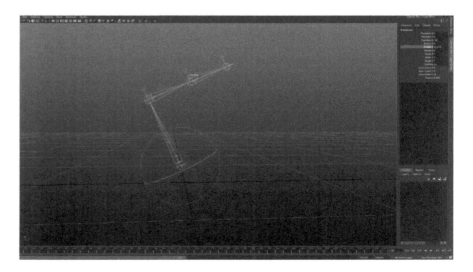

FIGURE 3.7 The joint orient offsets the alignment of the joint from the World. When you rotate the joint in the "gimbal," or Euler, you can see that it uses that offset alignment to calculate the rotations.

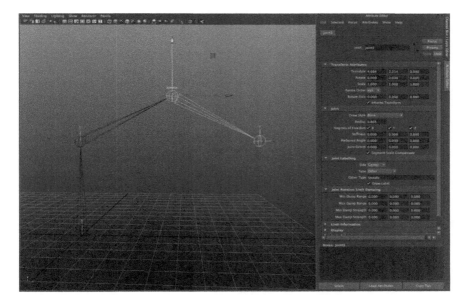

FIGURE 3.8   The selected "spindle" has Joint Orient values and rotation values of zero.

also rotate perfectly around its axis. You can see the action of a spindle axis in your Humerus, or shoulder joint, as it rolls in the socket. The only way to achieve this effect in a joint chain is to make sure that at least one axis of this chain in pointed down the bone exactly at the child joint.

In Figure 3.8 we can see that the layout of our arm contains some joints that aren't aligned with the world axis. But the joint labeled "spindle" is supposed to spin around its own axis, like a drill bit! If we rotate it based on its current Y rotation orientation, you will see the arm swing around the World Y-axis. But if we want this to rotate around its axis like a "spindle" or drill bit, we must orient one axis to aim directly at the child joint, which is the last joint in the chain. That way it will retain rotation values of zero in the local Euler XYZ channels, but it will rotate based on an offset that allows it to spin around its own axis as it relates to the child joint. This is what a "Joint Orient" is for.

Now, I know it's still not *totally* clear what the purpose of these joint orients really is, or how to change them. But just for laughs, let's look at Figure 3.9, where the joint orient is being set. If you look at the resulting alignment of the spindle joint, you will see that now the X-axis is aiming down the joint, toward the child. The Y-axis is now aiming at a 90° angle to that joint from the front perspective (actually using the positive Y-axis as a guide) and the

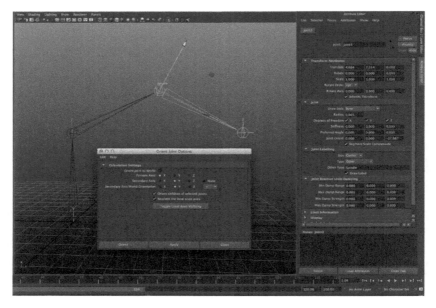

FIGURE 3.9 Now the joint has been oriented and it will rotate properly in a spindle manner.

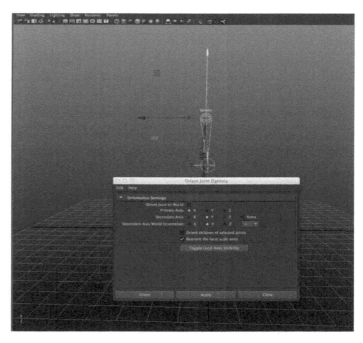

FIGURE 3.10 Orienting the joints will change the alignment based on several parameters.

Z-axis is actually now forming a 90° angle along the forward Z-axis, as you can see in Figure 3.10. All of these options are shown in the options dialogue of the Joint Orient Action, and we'll go over all these in just a bit.

Now, the whole point in setting the orient of this joint was to get the joint to spin around its axis evenly while retaining the values of zero in the Euler XYZ channel. And we have succeeded! If you look again at Figure 3.9, you will clearly see that by rotating our spindle joint in the local Euler X-axis, it will form a perfect arc around its length, just like a drill bit.

3.4 HOW DO YOU SET JOINT ORIENTS?

The Joint Orient action is a dialogue box in Maya where you can automatically set the orient of a joint, even if it is inside of a hierarchy, without changing the rotation of those joints. What this does is automatically set the joint orients of a joint (or chain of joints if you use the "Orient children of selected joints" options) based on a few parameters. Let's look at the "Orient Joint Options" box in some detail, as shown in Figure 3.11.

"Orient Joint to World" is the first option you will see. This will turn off all the axis options and set the Joint Orients to zero, which is to say that it will be oriented to the World.

"Primary Axis" is the axis that will be "aimed" at the child joint. In Figure 3.8 you can see that the spindle joint's X-axis is pointed toward the child joint. You have three options here, and whichever is the Primary axis will be aimed toward the child joint. The other two axes (in this case the Y and Z) will form right angles with the Primary Axis in one plane. That plane is dependent on the next two options we choose. *If* there is no child

FIGURE 3.11 The Joint Orient options dialogue.

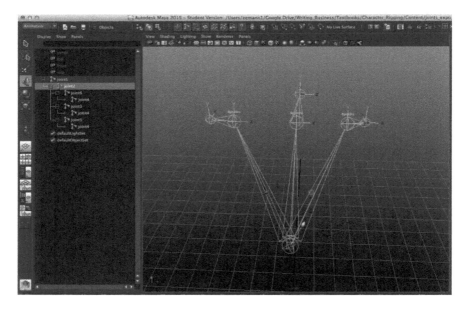

FIGURE 3.12 A multiple-sibling joint setup where the root of the three "fingers" has been oriented—since the joint to the left of the root is the first in the hierarchy order, it will be the one the parent joint orients its axis to.

joint (i.e., this is the last joint in the chain), then nothing will change for the selected joint, as there is no child of this joint for it to align itself to. *If* the joint you are orienting has more than one child (as in Figure 3.12), then the joint will orient itself to the first child joint in the hierarchy list order (which is visible by opening the Outliner and checking the order). Also something to note about the Joint Orient Action is that it will not work if any of the joints you want to orient have rotation values that are anything other than zero.

"Secondary Axis" indicates which of the remaining two axes you wish to use as a reference point. This is needed because there are three axes, and we only know the direction of one of them so far (the Primary Axis). *Now* we need to know where the other two axes will be aiming. If we can figure out the Secondary Axis direction, then we know where the third axis is by the process of elimination. This is a lot easier to understand when you look at the photograph of the "joint orient stick" the author has created to give you a better visual reference. You can see from Figure 3.13 that a human arm, when bent, presents a nonaligned chain of joints that we have to set up in order to rotate properly. The red section of the stick represents the X-axis, the green the Y-axis, and the blue the Z-axis. The rules of this alignment are simple— the Primary Axis runs down the length of the bone, aiming at the child

FIGURE 3.13   This is the joint orient stick. You can see that the Y as Primary Axis points down from the shoulder to the elbow, and the X-axis as the Secondary Axis points toward the positive Z-axis, which would make the Secondary World Axis Orientation the +Z!

(in this case the Humerus or shoulder joint and the elbow), and the other two axes form perfect right angles with one another *and* the Primary Axis. All we have to do now is to rotate the Joint Orient Stick around the Primary Axis and we can determine the planes upon which the Humerus will rotate. The Secondary World Axis Orientation simply uses a World Axis alignment to try and line up the Joint Orient Stick properly. Since our real-life model, and subsequent character model in 3D is going to be in the "A-Stance," with thumbs down, we can use the Positive Z-Axis as a Secondary World Axis Orientation, as you can see in Figure 3.14. The Secondary Axis will do its best to align itself with the positive Z-axis, which will result in the Y-axis of the joint poking straight toward the viewer from the Front view. If we had chosen the Z-axis as the Secondary Axis, it would be the Z-axis pointing forward instead of the Y. Technically it doesn't really matter which axis is pointing where, as long as you know how they are arranged *and* you set the Joint Rotation Order accordingly. Doing all this properly takes some practice, but becomes easy with repetition. One nice thing is that every joint doesn't have to have the same orient axes or rotation when working strictly in Maya; however, in various game engines these things are necessary to be set in a certain way (for instance, in Unity the Joint Rotation Order is default at ZXY and in Maya it is XYZ), so often you will be limited to one way of doing things.

FIGURE 3.14   This is the same as Figure 3.13, however, the Secondary World Axis Orientation has now been changed to +X, which aims the X-axis toward the character's left and the Z-axis away from the viewer. Contrary to rumor, I use this stick to teach students how joint orients work, and not beat them with it—unless they get it wrong.

3.5 WHAT IS THE BEST CONFIGURATION TO SET UP JOINT ORIENTS?

There is no absolutely proper configuration for setting joint orients. You do yourself a favor making them line up with the cardinal axes as much as possible, but it really depends on the thing you are trying to set a skeleton for. As you will see in the next chapter, the whole purpose of this operation is to set up a proper movement system for your character, and *that* should be the primary goal. So make sure the elbow rotates like an elbow, and in the correct plane. Some game engines and studios have certain rules to follow, especially when the animation engines depend on certain transform matrices being in certain orders, so that will often guide your setup.

Also, don't forget that the Joint Orient Action tool is only an *automated* way of setting joint orients. You can certainly tweak them all you want yourself! And indeed you might need to if you are trying to set up a skeleton for an insect, dragon, or any other nonstandard animal that doesn't conform to the basic bipedal movement system. Manually changing the joint orient can be done after orienting it, mostly by adjusting the value of the Joint Orient on the spindle axis (otherwise the spindle won't work properly).

3.6 HOW DO JOINT ORIENTS RELATE TO ROTATION ORDER?

Once you have set up the Joint Orients, the Rotation Order will operate just as it did for us previously. Only *now* it will work with the orientation you specified in the Joint Orients, instead of just offset from the World axis alignment. We will see how this makes a difference in the next chapter when we begin constructing a skeleton for a character.

3.7 DOES TRANSLATING JOINTS AFFECT THE JOINT ORIENT AT ALL?

Yes, yes, yes, yes!!! *Never* translate a joint, unless it is the root joint, inside of a hierarchy if you want your joint orients to remain correct! Joints inside a hierarchy are almost exclusively rotated, unless there is some special case occurring. *If* you translate a joint for some reason *after* you have oriented the joints *that joint* and *its parent joint will both have to be reoriented*. This happens often when adjusting joint positions for deformation purposes, and it must be addressed or your skeleton will be oriented completely incorrectly, and, hence, animate incorrectly. This is a huge novice blunder, and it's very common to see this in amateur demo reels and character rigs set up by nonriggers. Rotating a joint, however, does not change the joint orient, because it simply "offsets" the value of the orient by whatever value is in the rotation channel.

CHAPTER 4

Primary Skeleton

4.1 WHAT IS A SKELETON?

Now that you are comfortable with Hierarchies, Euler Rotations, and Joint Orients, it's time to delve into the whole purpose for having all this stuff in a 3D engine: skeletons. A skeleton is a multitiered, hierarchy of joints that represent in some way the manner in which your intended model or object is going to move. It doesn't always *have* to be in regard to an actual character; in fact, skeletons and hierarchical movements can be applied to all sorts of mechanics and other properties of 3D movement. The important thing that you need to know is how multiple rotations and translations are managed in a hierarchy, and *what* exactly you'll be doing with it.

4.2 WHAT ARE SKELETONS USED FOR?

There are two primary functions for a skeleton; to animate using Kinematics and to deform a model using skinning methods. The first we will be exploring in this chapter, and the second we will be examining later on in the book. Without skeletons it is completely possible to animate based on a hierarchy, but the joint properties, especially joint orient, allows us to do this much easier than simply using parenting.

4.3 WHAT IS FORWARD KINEMATICS?

Forward Kinematics refers to the most important concept in animating a skeletal hierarchy. This is the principle that rotating a joint will never change the *position* of that joint, in world or local space, but it *will* change the world

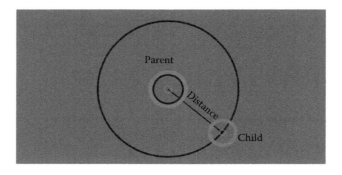

FIGURE 4.1   Forward Kinematics is the relationship of the Child translating in the World around the Parent axis.

position of its children, based on an arc around the parent joint. Figure 4.1 is 2D representation of this concept. The parent joint, represented by the larger circle, has a pivot point in its center. The child joint, represented by the smaller circle, is translated in world space based on its parent's pivot. This means that when the parent joint rotates, the child joint *translates*, in an arc, around the parent. Figure 4.2 illustrates the 90° rotation of this arc. Notice that the distance, as indicated, between the two joints, never changes. So the child joint retains its local *position*, but changes its world position.

Forward Kinematics is how you move your body, provided it is freely floating in space or water. Your muscles twitch, stretching or pulling, and they pull tendons that rotate your joints. I say this happens in a perfectly "free-floating" environment because when you are connected to another solid body, say your feet to the ground, there are physical forces that change things (more on this later).

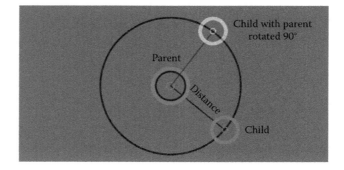

FIGURE 4.2   This illustrates the arc that the Child Node translates around in World Space. Note that the local space, in terms of the distance relative to the Parent Node, hasn't changed at all!

4.4 WHAT DIFFERENT POSES ARE CHARACTERS MODELED IN, AND HOW DOES THAT AFFECT THE SKELETON?

There are several "bind poses" or "stances" that a character may be modeled in. Mostly 3D bipedal characters are modeled a certain way, but there are all sorts of subtle variations upon each specific type. There is the "T-Stance," which has the arms and the legs as close to align with the World Axis as possible. This is *always* the preferred way to *rig* a character, due to the ease of joint alignment, but it's not really the best way to *deform* a character, which is more important to the appearance of the end result. The shoulders have the most difficulty in evaluating deformations and having them outstretched in a T-Pose is not going to give you a very natural neutral appearance. Having the legs in a perfect T-Pose is harder on the modeler, especially when the thighs are thick enough to cross the center of the character along the Z-axis. It's also very poor for modeling and deforming the crotch area. Figure 4.3 is an example of a T-Pose.

The A-stance is by far the more common character model stance, as illustrated in Figure 4.4. The arms are at ~45° angles toward the ground, making the fold of the armpit and the rounded area of the upper shoulder very natural in a neutral stance, or with the arms by the sides, as most of our human physical actions will take place somewhere in

FIGURE 4.3 The T-Stance, which is a great pose for rigging but a bad one for deformation. Notice how awkward the shoulders are?

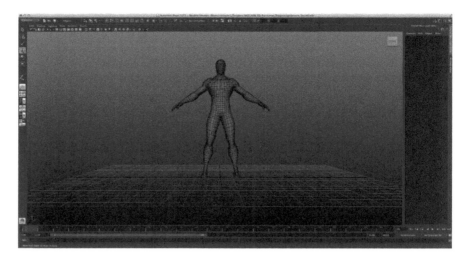

FIGURE 4.4   The proper A-Stance, with ankles aligned to the leg.

this range. The legs are also rotated at a slight angle making an "A" shape. This is *much* harder to rig, since the legs don't align with the world, but better for deformation. One thing you will notice about Figure 4.4 is that the ankles are *aligned with the knees*, and not with the ground! This is the correct A-Pose, and makes life infinitely better for the rigger. When the ankles are oriented with the ground plane, or World Y-axis, but the legs are in an A-Pose, it means that the legs are "straight" on two axes, and that is going to be problematic later on. It's possible to correct for this in a rig, but much more difficult, although as a rigger you will often get models that are set up like this and will have to deal with it in some way.

The examples in Figures 4.3 through 4.6 are just some variations on bipedal "modeled" poses. There are tons of variations on the hip rotation, ankle alignment, and knee/elbow flex levels. Ankles and wrists are also highly variable, depending on the modeler, the output, and a million other factors. One of the things that will help you, the rigger, to get as good a rig as possible from the start is to be able to evaluate the model upon receiving it (or if you're modeling it, while modeling). Remember, the modeler is often more of a sculptor than an anatomist—he/she will spend a lot of time getting it to *look* right over getting it to *move* right. That's your job! But the job is a lot harder if the modeler is not using proper skeletal alignment.

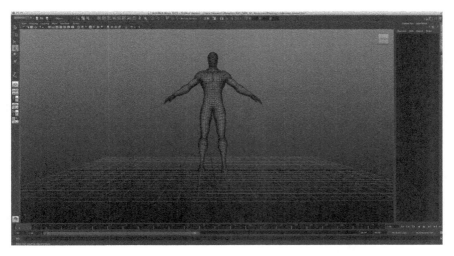

FIGURE 4.5 The improper A-Stance, with the ankles aligned to the ground plane. Notice the odd angles as illustrated? This is technically correct in terms of anatomy if you are standing on the ground, but more difficult to rig properly.

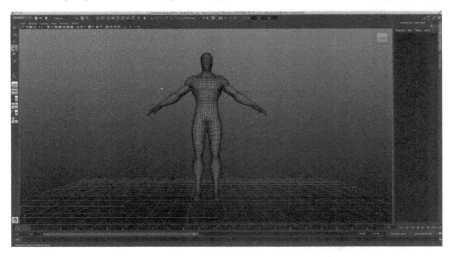

FIGURE 4.6 A hybrid setup with A-Stance arms and T-Stance legs (my personal favorite).

4.5 WHAT IS SKELETAL ALIGNMENT AND HOW DOES IT RELATE TO THE CHARACTER MODEL?

Skeletal alignment, as it pertains to the character model you need to build a skeleton for, is of vital importance if you are going to set it up correctly. The important thing is to understand the major parts of the body, as you will be constructing them, and how they are aligned and operate. Each part of the human body has its unique method of movement.

Let's start with the torso. The torso can be divided into four parts; three solid objects and one flexible center. The solid elements, as you can see in Figure 4.7, are simply planes upon which you can draw straight angles with *different* forward vectors. As you can see the hips, ribcage, and head all represent a solid mass of bone that points in a single direction as a whole— you turn to the right or left with your head, torso, or entire body (the legs with the hips). All three of those elements can be angled in different directions. The soft part, holding them all together, is the midsection, which has only the flexible spinal column to take up all that slack from the other solid masses. We're lucky it's so flexible and strong, because if you think about it there's an entire section from your bellybutton to your sternum that's only supported by that long, straight collection of vertebrae. This is probably why lower back problems cause so many people so much pain—it keeps the entire skeletal mass of your upper body upright! (Figure 4.8)

The point of getting all this information is that we have to construct a skeleton, based on some simple rotational joints, that handles all of this complexity. By narrowing down the prominent players in human movement we can use as few joints as possible in our structure. So at this point we know we need joints for the Hips, Upper Torso, and Head for "animation" purposes. We will also have to put at least one in between the Upper torso and Hips

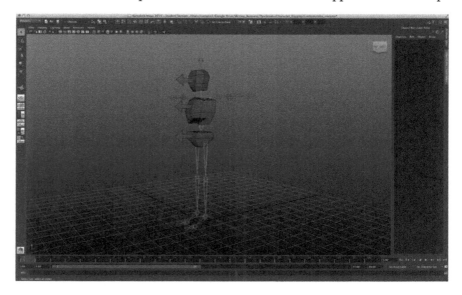

FIGURE 4.7 **(See color insert.)** The major planes of the human vertical axis.

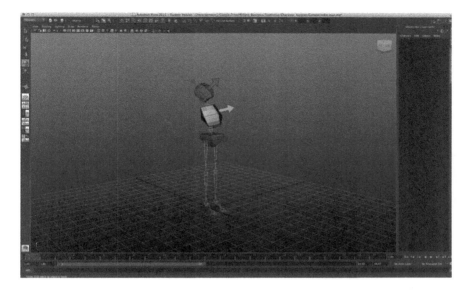

FIGURE 4.8 **(See color insert.)** These planes can be pointing in multiple directions due to the flexibility of the spine.

for "deformation" purposes. That extra joint is there for deformation stability (which we'll get into later). It is important to note here that in more sophisticated designs we have an animation skeleton and a deformation skeleton, one riding on top of the other, but that is fairly advanced. In Chapter 9 and the accompanying video tutorial there will be instructions on how to accomplish this. For now, we're creating the *minimal* skeleton to do all that work for us! It's more efficient, but we lose a lot of subtle deformation possibilities.

OK, now let's look at the legs. A leg consists of a hip socket-joint, which rotates in all three axes like all ball-and-socket joints, but the hip is *limited* in its movement. As you can see in Figure 4.9, the hip may rotate forward (your knee lifting upward toward your face) but it doesn't move back along that same angle very far (unless you do a *lot* of yoga). On the same principle, we can get the inside rotation angle of the hip (toward your other foot, crossing over the plumb line of your body) around 45°, but *nobody* is going very far in the opposite direction (unless you want to break your hip!) without rotating the hip in the socket (which frees it to move upward). Not even a ballerina. The hip rotates along its spindle axis a little bit, enough to roll your knee to the right or left (or do those ballerina *pliés* you're so fond of), but the range of motion for most of us non–ballet professionals is fairly limited. The reason for this is because we are bipedal and require the motion to be somewhat limited if we want to be effective at running in a forward vector. The flexibility is

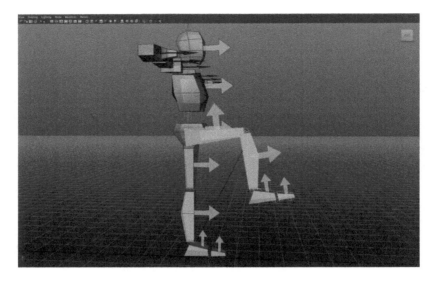

FIGURE 4.9 (**See color insert.**) The hip is the fulcrum of the upper leg, which rotates the furthest range of motion toward your belly.

still there, however, if we need to move laterally or even backward. In the animal kingdom, we have some of the most flexible and versatile bodies, which probably aid in our success as a species. Many animals are very specialized in their form of movement. Look at a dog, for example. They have extremely limited flexion in their hips and shoulders, but they can usually outrun us in a short distance, and if you've ever tried to catch a dog who doesn't want to be caught, you'll understand how convenient those four limbs on the ground can be. They can make rapid turns extremely fast. They have a specialized form of locomotion, but it limits their overall mobility.

Speaking of limited mobility—the knee is a hinge joint or a joint that *only* rotates in a single plane and that plane is perfectly aligned with the direction of the hip and ankle, forming a perfect triangle. That means that standing straight and flexing your knee *only* (don't cheat and twist your hip), it will always hit you in the butt. If you set up a leg properly with the skeleton and this *doesn't* happen—either the modeler or you are in error.

OK, *now* we get to the "foot." The foot is a particularly difficult problem in terms of rigging because it's what connects you to the ground! And when you're connected to the ground, the ground start making determinations about body alignments. The ankle is the first joint—it's actually a complex structure of three joints that meet near that bony protrusion (Malleolus). This combination of joints allows the ankle to rotate mainly on the World

X-axis, and, somewhat laterally, on the World Z-axis (assuming that the character is facing forward in the Z-axis). That's because it must give and flex with the full weight of your body as you thump down the street, pounding it into oblivion. These directions are controlled by gravity and your contact point with the earth—which means in essence your body pivots around your ankle/heel, which is what is known as a "closed kinematic system." If you are swimming or flying (wouldn't *that* be cool) you are using an "open" kinematic system, which means that you are rotating the ankle entirely based on willful control.

So the ankle, when connected to the ground, is always going to have its pivot axis, and therefore joint orient, aligned with the World Y-axis at the very least. Generally, if the character isn't doing anything special and we don't have a good reason to orient this joint, we can leave it oriented to the world. Why make our lives harder? In Figure 4.10, you can see this in operation, outlining the planes that the foot can rotate on. There are three more contact points with the ground possible; the ball, the toe, and the heel. We'll talk more about these later, but for the initial skeleton we just need the ball and toe, and those can retain their world orientation. Like the heel, they don't really need to be aligned to their children, since they won't be spinning on an axis. If you are using a setup where you *must* orient these joints with one axis aiming down the bone, it will still be fine since there are only two planes of rotation anyway.

FIGURE 4.10 **(See color insert.)** The planes of orientation related to the foot and ankle when the foot is planted on the ground.

So now we must undertake the toughest part of our basic skeleton: the shoulder! The problem with our shoulder is that we have a few extra bones up there to get all that awesome range of motion. Most animals, especially quadrupeds like dogs, don't have all that shoulder mobility that we have. The Clavicle, or shoulder joints, are adapted for walking on four legs, and even animals like bears that can stand upright and pick up stuff with their paws would have a *really* hard time making a free throw in basketball because they can't lift their arms over their head! What other animals have an easy time with this? You guessed it... primates! It makes sense, since we need that extra mobility to hang from tree limbs, throw things, and use tools. You see, our Humerus is a ball and socket, but a ball and socket joint doesn't really come with a full range of motion (unless you're a robot)—it just gives us a good range of motion in three axes. What's really special about our shoulders is that the Clavicle "lifts up" in order to allow that extra mobility so we can hang from the "monkey bars" at the playground (and now we know why they're called monkey bars). As the Clavicle lifts, the Humerus kind of "rolls under" so it can maneuver the arms to where you clasp your hands over your head. This is a tricky thing for a rigger to set up, since the natural mechanics are so much more complex than we can easily re-create in 3D, given the tools at our disposal. Now, there is absolutely a way to set up a complex, anatomically correct shoulder rig, but it's not really *necessary*. In 3D art, we need to make it *look* correct more than we need to make it a perfect anatomical representation.

The trick is to get the Clavicle joint, which is the parent of the Humerus joint, placed properly so that it functions as close to the human mechanic as possible. Here, the Clavicle joint is going to really represent the entire area of our skeletal anatomy that controls the shoulder hinge above the Humerus, which is the ball and socket joint. There are several joints in the pectoral girdle, including the Scapula, that are involved in the motion, but when setting up a basic skeleton the Clavicle is the important thing to get right, because it is the parent of the Humerus, and therefore controls the pivot from where it will rotate. As you can see in Figures 4.11 and 4.12, the Clavicle area is responsible for rotating in two axes (assuming your character is facing forward on the positive Z-Axis); aligned with the World Z-axis, which will control the lift of your shoulders, or shrugging action, and the hinge aspect, which rotates with the World X-axis, and would be what happens when you extend your arms fully forward or backward (clasping your hands behind your back). The Clavicle should not "roll" at all, so it doesn't need a spindle axis. In fact, assuming that you don't have

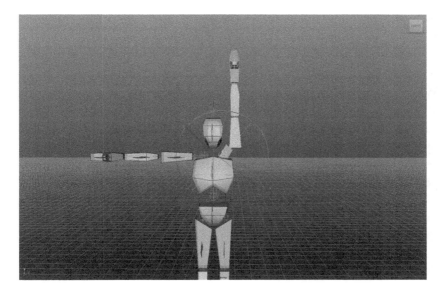

FIGURE 4.11 **(See color insert.)** Lifting the arms above the head requires the Clavicle to rotate in the World Z-axis here.

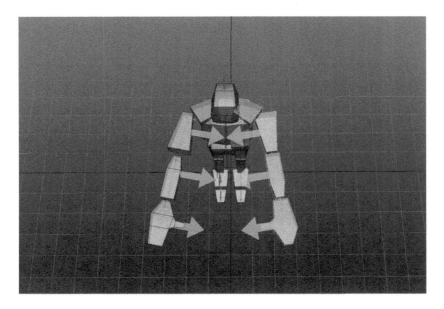

FIGURE 4.12 **(See color insert.)** The hinging of the Clavicle forward.

to orient all of the joints in your skeleton in any certain way, the Clavicle is best left oriented to the World axis in an upright biped.

Despite the fact that this hinge moves in positive and negative direction of both axes, let's not forget that the range of motion is fairly limited. When setting up for movement of your Clavicle, we need to put the joint at the pivot axis of the character's *real* Clavicle—this is for both mechanics and for deformation purposes. You can feel the pivot of your Clavicle by running your finger along your collar-bone toward your sternum (the center of your chest) until it pokes out a little, like a knob. *That* is the position from which the joint will rotate. It actually hinges from a more forward position than the center of the body, but because the scapula and the rest of the mechanisms for movement here kind of take up the slack, we want to move it slightly back from where the modeler has modeled the collar bone area. It greatly depends on your model, but the important thing is to avoid the "broken collarbone" look when the joint is rotated in the World-Y axis. If the joint is placed too far forward, as in Figure 4.13, it will cause the shoulder to look dislocated, or as if it's hinging way too far forward, even though this is the actual point of the bone in your real body. So we want to put it about 15% forward from the center cord of the body, which is characterized by the Y-axis of the spine. If we put it in the middle, often the shoulder will look wrong when pulling the arms back.

FIGURE 4.13 **(See color insert.)** Don't let the Clavicle node be too far in front of the body midaxis, like it is here.

Don't forget, however, that this hinging action on the World Y-axis for our character is *limited*. We don't need a whole lot of rotation to get the intended effect. Don't' break your character's shoulder! Negative 30° to 30° on the World Y-axis is a good range limit to keep in mind.

The Humerus is a ball and socket joint, so it *must* be oriented to its child! Even though we actually use a twist node (or several) to do the twisting, we need this joint lined up with the child. The Humerus, being a ball and socket joint, has freedom on all three axes. And it has the most range of motion of any joint in the body on all three axes. Don't forget that like the leg, the arm must have a perfect triangular alignment with the Humerus, elbow, and wrist in the plane of the elbow rotation, which is fixed to a single Vector. You can see this alignment is perfect in Figure 4.14, because our character was set up in the T-Pose. But in Figure 4.15, you can clearly see the "bent" angle between the Humerus and the wrist, because the modeler created the character in the "relaxed" pose, or the A-Stance. In this case this alignment is incorrect. You can adjust the positions of the joints slightly in order to match this alignment as much as possible, but sometimes the modeler needs to reassess the flow of geometry as well. It's always a give and take between the two.

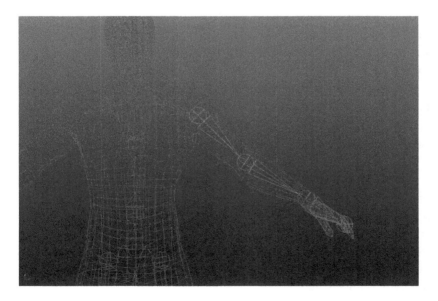

FIGURE 4.14   The arm is not modeled correctly, therefore, you can clearly see that the proper joint alignment is off between the shoulder, elbow, and the wrist (note that the arm came this way; it was not altered from the original state in any way).

FIGURE 4.15 This is the proper skeletal alignment. In this case I would hand it back to the modeler and let them fix it, or try to adjust it myself.

The wrist is an interesting area of the arm—although it *seems* like it can turn in all three axes, in reality what we have are two joints in the forearm; the Ulna and Radius, which twist around one another like a towel being wrung out. This allows us to roll the wrist without needing a ball-and-socket joint! Now, once again you can create a genuine Ulna/Radius rig if you want, but what we really need is for just the action to *look* correct. Later on we will be discussing *twist* nodes and how to create them and control them. For now we will pass over this and just concentrate on getting the wrist correct.

The wrist, which doesn't actually roll on its own, as we discussed, nevertheless *must* have a roll axis properly oriented. *but*, since we have multiple children branching from it, how do we ensure that it's oriented properly? In this case, we can zero out the joint orients for this particular joint and it will achieve perfect alignment with its parent joint, the elbow, which is exactly what we want. IF we try to orient a joint with multiple children, the first one in the hierarchical order will be used for the Primary Axis, which isn't always what we want. So in this case if we just zero out those Wrist joint orients, it will set up the wrist properly for us. The wrist needs to bend with ~90° of mobility and rotate laterally with about ~30° of mobility.

4.6 HOW DO I ASSESS A CHARACTER MODEL FOR SKELETAL ALIGNMENT?

For most bipedal characters the best way to assess the skeletal alignment is to set up a skeleton based on the geometry, and then start parenting the joints in the chains. My rules of thumb for good alignment are that the spine should be a perfectly straight line at 90° to the ground plane and go through the center of the body exactly through to the top of the head. The neck will usually be a tad off-center. The hip to the ankle through the knee should be a perfectly flat triangle along the plane that the knee will rotate, and you know which plane that will be because the knee is a hinge joint and can only rotate on a single axis. *If* the ankle is aligned with the leg, it will bend in perfect alignment with the knee, but *if* the ankle is aligned with the ground plane, it will be aligned with the World Y-axis. The Clavicle and Humerus should be very close to level on the Y-axis, with some give in either direction depending on the model. The Humerus, elbow, and wrist should be a perfect triangle in the vector that the elbow rotates, with the thumb hitting the Humerus perfectly.

4.7 LESSON 1: CREATING THE BASIC SKELETON

4.7.1 Step 1: Load the File

Open the human model file with the geometry. You will note that this model has been scaled to ~6 ft tall, or 1.8 m. When rigging characters it is best to try and conform to the real-world dimensions, since scaling a character rig, while possible, can be a dicey procedure for too many reasons to list here. The character model should always face forward on the Z-axis, with the left hand on the positive X-axis (Figure 4.16).

4.7.2 Step 2: Create the Template Joint

Now we need a Template Joint, or a joint that we can tweak the parameters of and copy it to generate all the others. Go to the Skeleton > Joint Tool, and open up the tool option box. Make sure that the joint orients are "Set to World" and use the grid-snap (x) key to set it on the grid (Figures 4.17 and 4.18).

4.7.3 Step 3: Expose the Joint Orients

Now that we have the template joint created, we need to change a few settings in order to have it be useful. Go to Window > General Editors > Channel Control in order to bring up the Channel Box control. This allows you to expose all those extra attributes not currently visible in the Channel Box. Select the Joint Orient X, Y, and Z from the list by highlighting them,

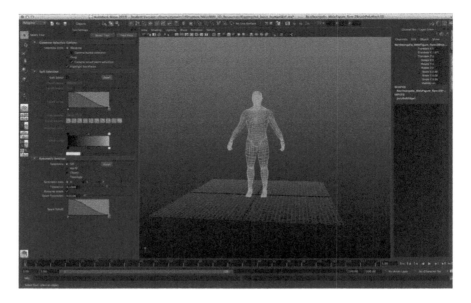

FIGURE 4.16   The character always faces forward on the Z-axis (Human model by 3D artist Ben DeAngelis).

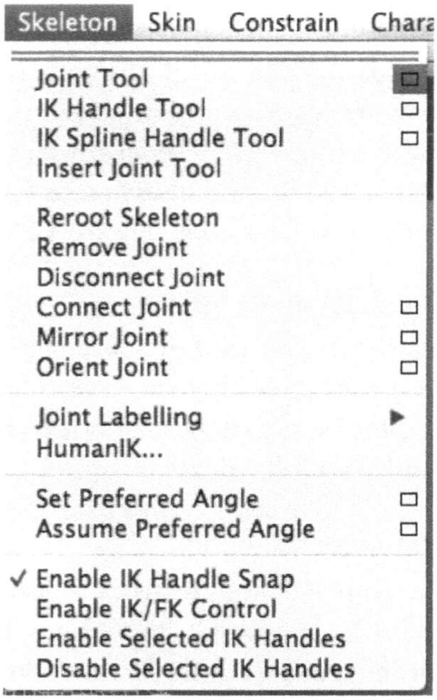

Skeleton	Skin	Constrain	Chara

Joint Tool ☐
IK Handle Tool ☐
IK Spline Handle Tool ☐
Insert Joint Tool

Reroot Skeleton
Remove Joint
Disconnect Joint
Connect Joint ☐
Mirror Joint ☐
Orient Joint ☐

Joint Labelling ▶
HumanIK...

Set Preferred Angle ☐
Assume Preferred Angle ☐

✓ Enable IK Handle Snap
Enable IK/FK Control
Enable Selected IK Handles
Disable Selected IK Handles

FIGURE 4.17   The Joint Tool in Maya.

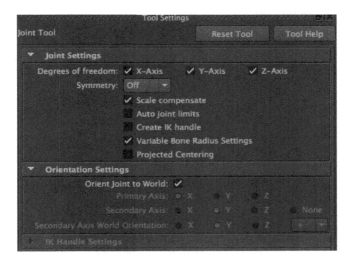

FIGURE 4.18   Make sure that Orient Joint to World is checked.

and then click on the button to the bottom left that moves them into the visible, but not keyable state! It will pop those values into the Channel Box so that we can see and edit them if need be (Figure 4.19).

4.7.4 Step 4: Create the Spine

Keep the Template Joint where it is, and Duplicate it using Edit > Duplicate. Now we will create the Torso. Use the duplicated joint to create the Hips and place them at the center of the pelvis, right below the belly button, and centered in the Z-axis of the character's body mass. Duplicate that joint again and move it straight up in the Y-axis, forming the Spine_1, which will reside right between the ribcage and the pelvis. This is not a "hard" joint, but more of a "twist" node in order to provide an anchor between the upper torso and lower torso deformation. Duplicate that joint and create Spine_2, which will represent the solid mass of the ribcage. It goes just about in the middle of the ribcage. Duplicate that again and move it straight up in the Y-axis, forming the Neck, right at the base of where the physical neck connects to the body. Duplicate this again and move it straight up on the Y-axis to where the bottom of the earlobe would be. This is the Head joint. Make sure that ALL the torso joints are aligned straight with the Y-axis and one another. There should be a slight offset with the core of the body and the neck, due to the curvature of the spine, which is fine. We can offset these joints later if need be, but I like to keep it completely straight to begin with (Figure 4.20).

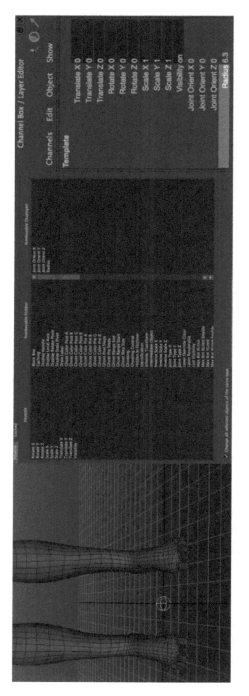

FIGURE 4.19   Exposing the Joint Orients in the Channel Box.

FIGURE 4.20   The torso skeleton joint positions. Notice it makes a straight line through the core of the body.

4.7.5 Step 5: Create the Legs

Now we need to do the limbs. Let's start with the legs. The first joint in the leg sequence, which we will derive from the Template joint once again, is the Femur, or Upper Leg. This is a ball-and-socket joint and must be free to rotate in all three axes. This joint goes just about where the crease of the upper thigh meets the top of the quadriceps—it should go somewhere in the middle of the body mass as well on the World Z-axis. The initial pose of the character here will determine a lot about the knee joint. In this instance, our character is in a shallow A-stance with the legs, which is deceptive because although it *seems* like a T-stance, it's not really since the alignment of the hip, knee, and ankle is somewhat off. So let's place the knee exactly in the middle of the "knob" of the knee and the ankle exactly in the center of the ankle joint. The ball and toe, however, will need to be in line with the ankle in whatever orientation the foot has been modeled in. In this case, it's fairly aligned along the World Z-Axis (as it should be), so we can copy the ankle to form the ball and the toe, moving them constrained to the Z-Axis. This way we *know* that the ankle, ball, and toe joints are aligned with the ground plane since our character is standing. Figures 4.21 and 4.22 illustrate

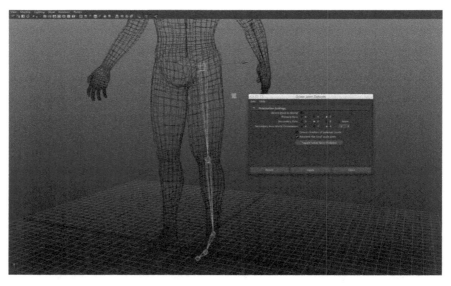

FIGURE 4.21   The leg, consisting of the Femur, Knee, Ankle, Ball, and Toes joints.

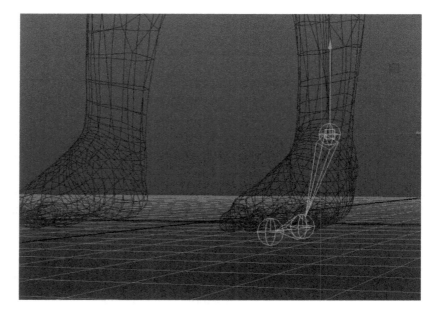

FIGURE 4.22   The ankle, ball, and toe are always aligned to the World Y-axis if the character is standing on the ground. The ball and toe joints are set to zero on the Y-axis for floor contact.

the proper alignment of a character in the A-stance with his feet aligned to the ground. Notice that the ball and toe joints are placed on the Y-axis zero! This is to make contact with the ground perfect and easy to keyframe values for.

4.7.6 Step 6: Orient the Leg Joints

Orienting the leg is the tricky part—it all depends on your rotation order! In this case, let's assume that we are adhering to an XYZ Euler Rotation Order, which is Maya's default (although by no means universal). In this case, we will want the spindle axis, or axis that the bone twists upon, to be the Primary Axis (in this case the Y-axis). This is a standard for many motion capture systems and game engines, although once again it's not necessarily universal. This also gives us the best results using the XYZ rotation order (Figure 4.23).

If I want the leg to operate properly in this position, I must choose to use the Y, X, +X settings for my Joint Orient options, in that order of: Primary Axis, Secondary Axis, and Secondary Axis World Orientation (see Figure 4.24). This gives us the perfect setup! Usually the X-axis is set to be the primary physical action of the joint in question or the one with the most range of motion. The Z-axis is generally the secondary axis of rotation. This is a general rule, although you might not always be able to do it this way. As long as the Y-axis is the Primary axis for all joints and the rotation order is consistent, everything will be fine (Figure 4.25).

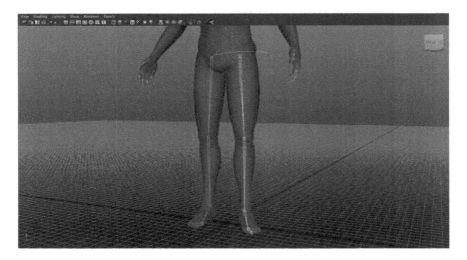

FIGURE 4.23 **(See color insert.)** The twisting of the leg from the Femur.

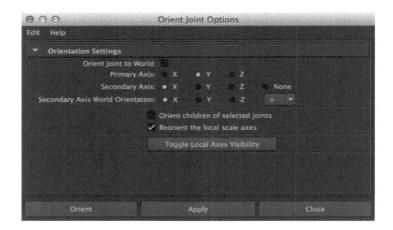

FIGURE 4.24 The Y-Axis was chosen as the Primary Axis, and then the X as the Secondary and the +X as the Secondary Axis World Orientation.

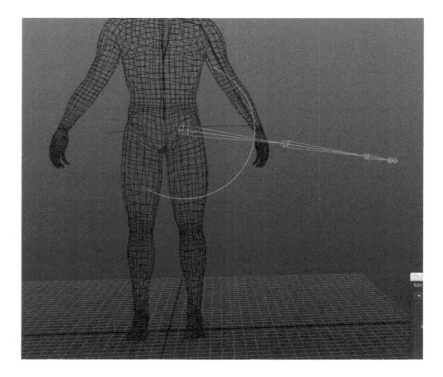

FIGURE 4.25 This is not a very likely position, so I put the Z-axis Orientation in this direction.

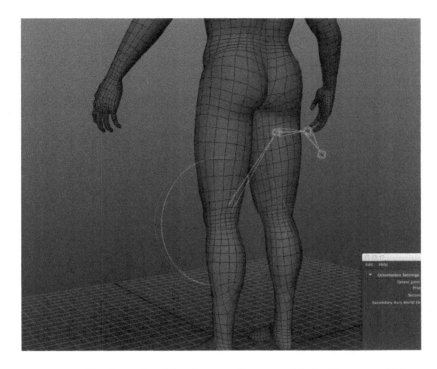

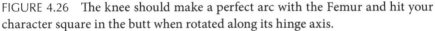

FIGURE 4.26   The knee should make a perfect arc with the Femur and hit your character square in the butt when rotated along its hinge axis.

Always check that leg alignment by rotating the knee in a single Euler Axis that represents the hinge direction of the knee. If you have set it correctly, it should rotate perfectly into the plane of the Femur. You can see this test in Figure 4.26.

The ankle, ball, and toe joints are a lot easier to deal with. They stay oriented to the World! When you are standing on the ground, the rest of your body actually rotate *around* the joint nearest the point of contact, like your ankle. So there is no reason or advantage in orienting those joints, unless for some reason you have to. Now you *must* orient the Y down the joint; using the Y, X, +X orientation will work just fine. Even though the alignment isn't with the World Axis, these joints will be using IK, which will be doing most of the work when they rotate.

4.7.7 Step 7: Create the Arms

OK, let's move on to the arm! First, we need to position the Clavicle. The Clavicle, as we learned, is responsible for hinging and creating the tremendous amount of flexibility we have in our arms. We can place the joint right where those collar bone points stick out on the character model. Then we want to sink it in to the character mass a little for deformation purposes. The Humerus comes next, and that we want right where that ball and socket is for a normal human—somewhere in-between the armpit and the top of the deltoid! The elbow goes right in the fold of the actual elbow and the wrist right in the center of the wrist area geometry (we're skipping the fingers for brevity). Just like the Femur to the Ankle, the Humerus to the Wrist is a perfect triangle along one plane. The elbow, when bent, should hook perfectly into the armpit—think about doing "The Funky Chicken" dance and you'll get the idea. We want that line to be straight! (Figures 4.27 through 4.29)

4.7.8 Step 8: Orient the Arm Joints

Now we will set the joint orients for our arm skeleton. The Clavicle doesn't need to be oriented to anything but the world. Why? Because it only pivots two ways—forward around the Y-Axis or "up" around the Z-axis, and both of these happen to correspond to the World alignment. Once again, why bother orienting it unless we have to? There's no advantage to it. The Humerus, on the other hand, most definitely needs

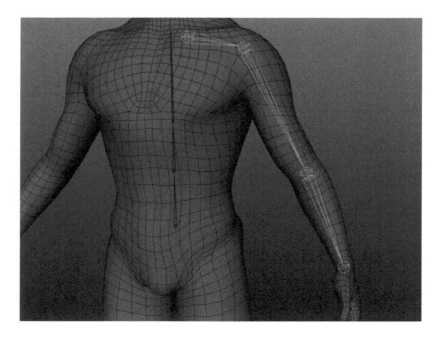

FIGURE 4.27 The arm joints from the front.

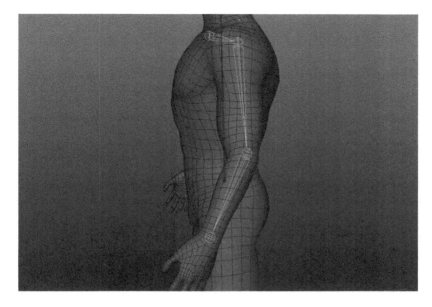

FIGURE 4.28   The arm joints from the side.

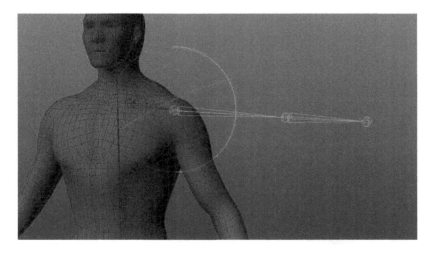

FIGURE 4.29   The gimbal lock would occur if the Humerus went any higher, but the Clavicle is what does that!

to be oriented to its child node, the elbow, in order to make a proper spindle axis and to create the elbow alignment planes. Once again, as I did with the Femur, I will use the Y-axis as my Primary axis, the X as my secondary, and the X-Positive as my secondary world axis orientation. This gives me a similar setup to the Femur, in which both the secondary action axis (in this case the rotation up and down) *and* the spin axes are on before the main axis rotation (the forward and back motion). So the X-axis will allow a full range of motion, aligned with the direction of the arm, regardless of how the other two Euler Channels are changed. The Y-axis, which is in the middle of the Rotation Order, should be the plane *least* likely to cause Gimbal flip, as you can see in Figure 4.30, the Y-axis of the Humerus really never goes further than 180°, making it safe to leave this in the middle.

Next, try to orient the elbow the same as the Humerus. In this case, we will choose Y, X, +Z because it gives us a better match for an axis to be perpendicular to the elbow and the Humerus joint. Once again, it would be nice if we could get the main rotation axis to be X, but in this case the Z works better. As long as that Y-axis is aimed down the join it shouldn't be a problem.

Double check your elbow rotation on the Z-axis to make sure that it's aligned! I can see that my model isn't perfectly aligned on that plane but it's close. You will rarely find a perfect alignment here, between the Humerus, Elbow, and Wrist. Modelers tend to have the forearm slightly

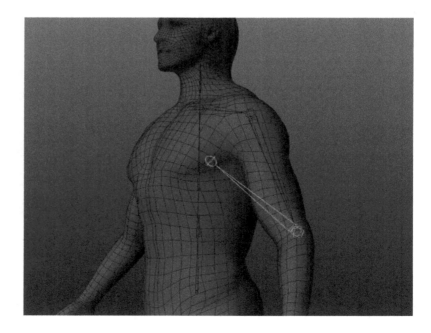

FIGURE 4.30   Check that elbow alignment!

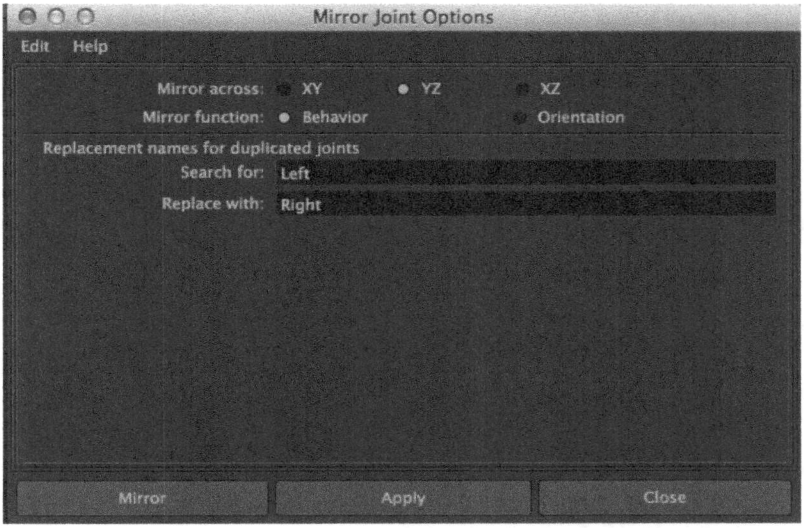

FIGURE 4.31   The Mirror Joint options. Notice I went ahead and renamed "Left" to "Right," making life infinitely easier for me down the road when I need to know which joint is which.

twisted to make the stance more "natural," but often offset the alignment a little. Most of the time, a little bit of correction will be needed in the deformation (Figure 4.31).

4.7.9 Step 9: Mirror the Limbs

OK, now that we have the left arms and legs set, adjusted, and oriented, we need to do this for the right side of the body! But don't get exasperated, we have a nice easy way to mirror all this stuff to the other side. All we have to do is use the Mirror Joints tool, on the YZ plane, and make sure we have "Behavior" checked, as in Figure 4.32. Behavior and Orientation are basically asking you which way you want to flip the axes—I almost always use Behavior.

Now you've done it! You have a basic skeleton, oriented and aligned properly! This is honestly one of the hardest things to get right from the bottom up for beginning riggers, so you should feel good about your progress so far. Many projects suffer down the road from improper alignment and poor planning for joint orients and rotation order, problems which could be avoided very early on. Now that everything is set up correctly, the rest of the work we must do is easier (Figures 4.33 through 4.41).

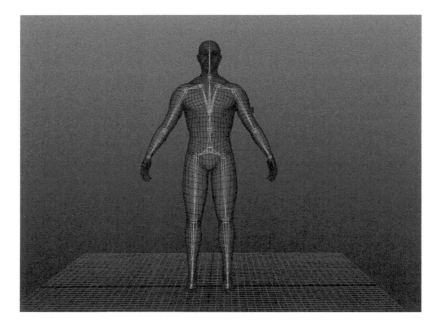

FIGURE 4.32   The entire basic skeleton.

FIGURE 4.33   The range of human motion for the rear rotation of the Femur.

FIGURE 4.34   Lifting the Femur toward the body.

FIGURE 4.35   The outside rotation, or abduction of the Femur, away from the body.

FIGURE 4.36 The abduction of the Femur toward the body, to the inside—notice how much less mobility there is here than to the outside?

FIGURE 4.37 The maximum lifting of the Humerus. Any more lift and the arms require the Clavicle to lift in order to get the arms over the head.

FIGURE 4.38 The Clavicle, lifting to allow for the Humerus to roll under and raise the arms over the head.

FIGURE 4.39 The Humerus lifting as the arm points forward.

FIGURE 4.40   The backward range of motion of the Humerus.

FIGURE 4.41   The full backward range of motion of the arm. Notice how the Clavicle has hinged back to increase the mobility?

CHAPTER 5

Intermediate Skeleton Setup

N OW THAT WE HAVE gone through the major joints and the proper placement, alignment, and hierarchy, we need to take a look at two more things: joint orient and joint rotation order. These are all aspects of creating the total single-skeleton package. The joint orients set up the direction of movement and the rotation order sets up the proper *order* of movement.

5.1 HOW DO I ORIENT MY JOINTS PROPERLY? HOW DO I DETERMINE ROTATION ORDER?

Joint orient values and Rotation Orders are a vital part of character rigging and setup and an often-overlooked one. There are a lot of modern "auto-rigging" solutions that kind of "skip over" this stuff because all of those systems are dependent on your character being in the T-Stance, which makes it easier to create a one-size-fits-all rigging system for any character. Mecanim, used by Unity3D, and HumanIK, used by Autodesk, are two such systems, and they work really well as a universal retargeting system. There's no reason you can't use your own skeleton and rig as part of one of those systems, however, and indeed you might often have to, especially when you are rigging a model that isn't built on a T-Stance (which isn't really optimal for deformation anyway).

Joint Orients and Rotation Orders should be addressed together, since they affect one another. It's hard to give anyone an absolute method for setting these up—often you will be limited to one path or another depending on your development constraints. For instance, Maya is a Y-up world, but Unreal Engine is Z-up. Unity3D has a ZXY Rotation Order. Several proprietary game engines I have worked with required (or were optimized for) Y as the Primary Axis. For all these reasons, it's really difficult to create a hard-and-fast rule for orienting the joints properly and setting the Rotation Order. Generally you will be fixed in *one* of these areas—that is to say that you will only have one rotation order to work with or only one Primary Axis you can use. Whichever of these two options you are constrained to will determine the choices in the other area. What matters most is the end result of your setup—how the joints rotate, in what plane, and what order the Euler channels are evaluated (which will really help smooth out your animations and prevent gimbal lock). If you happen to be doing all your work in Maya for the sake of a rendered animation, then you get the ultimate flexibility to use any combination of Joint Orient and Rotation order that you want, on a per-joint basis. This is ideal, but not usually a possibility when you are dealing with any real-time output, like for a game or VR-type application. Then you are almost always constrained by the limitations of the 3D engine that you are exporting to.

Since the most commonly and consistently locked attribute I have experienced is Rotation Order, I am going to work from the assumption in the following discussion on Joint Orients that the Rotation Order is set to Maya's default of XYZ. You can see in Figure 5.1 the setting I will use for *all* joints in this skeleton. Once again, I have to stress that in the absence of any strict guidelines, you can have any combination of Joint Orients and Rotation Orders you like—but usually you're constrained to one method or another. I'm simply using the XYZ because it is the default rotation of Maya. This provides a solid guideline to move forward with the proper orientation of the joints so that we avoid problems down the road.

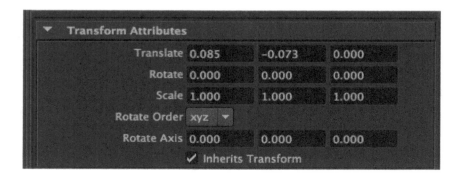

FIGURE 5.1   The Rotation Order is XYZ, which is the default Maya value.

With that in mind, we can now look at the joints that we will need to be orienting in order to make their alignment correct. For a human character, I try to adhere to some fairly hard-set rules in order to avoid confusion and assist the rigging process. The general rule of thumb is that, in the case of the XYZ rotation order, the Y-axis is the "spin" axis, the X-axis is the primary movement axis, and the Z-axis is the secondary movement axis.

The spine is easy: it's already oriented! Since we're bipeds without tails (as opposed to bipeds *with* tails, like a dinosaur), our spine should be perfectly aligned with the perpendicular angle of the ground! If your character isn't a hunchback or a stooped, old man, then we shouldn't have to do a thing with the orients from the root to the head—they should be straight up and down with the Y-axis. This not only saves you time and energy, but it makes the spine twist and rotate properly too.

The leg is the first major concern. One of the issues with the legs is that the hip–knee–ankle alignment can be very poorly set in the model, which will throw off our orientation if it's not addressed (as we discussed earlier). If we use the standard rule of thumb, the Primary Axis will be Y, the Secondary Axis will be X, and the Secondary World Axis Orientation will be +X, as you can see in Figure 5.2. This combination *should* work perfectly for the hip and knee joint in a bipedal character using the T-Stance or A-Stance, provided nothing weird is going on in the positions of the leg joints.

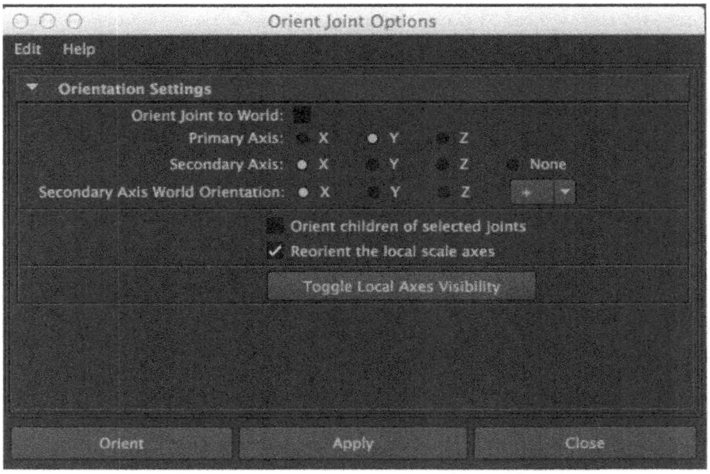

FIGURE 5.2   The Joint Orient Settings in Maya. The Primary Axis aims down the bone to the Child, becoming the twist axis. The Secondary Axis is the main rotation action for the joint and the Secondary Axis World Orientation is which Vector we want to aim that Secondary Axis, which is the positive X in this case.

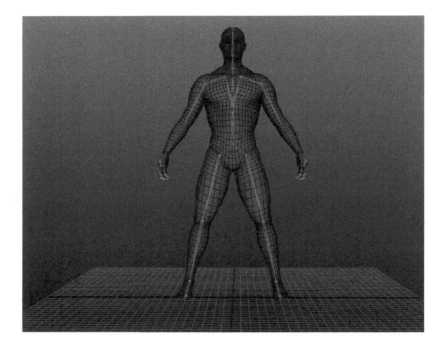

FIGURE 5.3   **(See color insert.)** Legs are wide, but ankles are aligned with the leg.

The ankle, ball, and toe joints present a unique scenario. IF the A-stance has the feet angled to match the alignment of the legs, as in Figure 5.3, we need to make the alignment of those joints match up with the hip–knee perfectly. But *if* the character is in the typical A-stance where the feet are standing on the ground (as in Figure 5.4), we actually don't want to orient them at all, since they must be aligned with the world axis in order to have the ground plane perpendicular to the foot. Most human-based characters are modeled with the feet planted on the ground, which means that, provided the foot is facing forward on the Z-axis, it should be perfectly aligned with the World axes. One of the problems with this is that it doesn't really conform to our Y-down-the-joint guideline. If we *must* orient the ankle and ball joints to the child joint with the Y-axis (or any other axis), there really isn't much we can do about it, but the rotations when animated aren't going to be a pure, single Euler axis. The good news is that these joints are almost always going to be processed with Inverse Kinematics of some kind to keep them planted on the ground, or using raw motion capture information, which in either case makes the proper alignment to the ground a moot point. But this is a problem with the A-stance in the legs, as I have already discussed, when

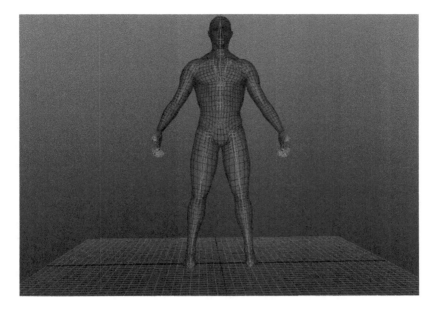

FIGURE 5.4 **(See color insert.)** Legs are wide, but the feet are firmly planted on the ground. This means the ankle, ball, and toe are good to go with World Axis alignments as they are—no orients needed.

the feet are planted on the ground, which is why I *always* prefer the T-stance for the legs. Then you don't have to worry about it! The constraints of your output will always guide your decisions in this regard.

If the foot for some reason is angled at 45°, that should mean that the character's leg is rotated outward (like a bowl-legged cowboy or clown) and this requires that the entire leg's orientation be completely different (and usually requires customization on a per-joint basis).

Now that the leg has been oriented, we can look at our arms' structure. The Clavicle is a joint that only rotates in two planes—no spin necessary! If you're not in need of aiming the Y down the joint for a particular reason, then I leave the Clavicle oriented to the World. This means that the Z-rotation is the "lifting" action of the Clavicle (or shoulder shrug) and the Y-rotation is the squeezing action for when you pull your shoulder blades together. Just a side note, if you absolutely need to orient the joints for pipeline reasons, you can insert a "dummy joint" in-between the Clavicle and the Humerus, which keeps the world alignment of the Clavicle but makes sure it's Primary Axis aims down to the child joint. This keeps the alignment intact and adheres to the rules of whatever pipeline you're using (usually Y down the bone). You can see an example of this in Figures 5.5 and 5.6.

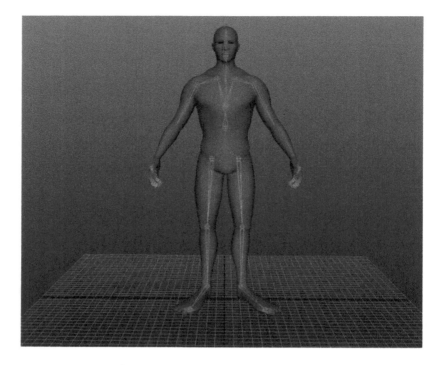

FIGURE 5.5 Since this character's frog-like legs are externally rotated, the standard Secondary Axis World Orientation won't give us good results.

OK, now that we have the Clavicle all figured out, we can get to the Humerus, elbow, and the wrist. These are very important orients to get right! The Humerus has 3° of rotation, and so we will need to make sure that it's rotating properly or there could be major repercussions down the road. Always try out the "standard" setup for Orients first—Y, X, X for an XYZ Rotation Order. You can see that this works just fine with our character's Humerus as modeled in Figure 5.7. But there's one big problem! It doesn't work with the elbow joint nearly as well. The reason for this is that the elbow, wrist, and Humerus alignment isn't perfect, plus the elbow isn't really lined up with the World X-axis. We can fix this in one of two ways—custom edit our joint orient values or just try a different Joint Orient setup. In this case, Y, X, and +Z (instead of +X) gives us better results (Figures 5.8 and 5.9). The primary action of the joint, the bending of the elbow, will be on the Z-axis now, but the elbow only rotated on one axis anyway and it still conforms to our Y-down-the-joint standard!

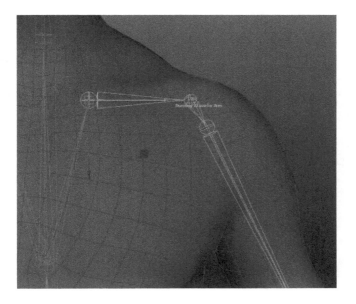

FIGURE 5.6 **(See color insert.)** The "dummy" joint preserving the basic alignment of the Clavicle while adhering to the Y-down-the-bone guideline. It's only
necessary if you have a pipeline which requires it; otherwise just leave the Clavicle
oriented to the world.

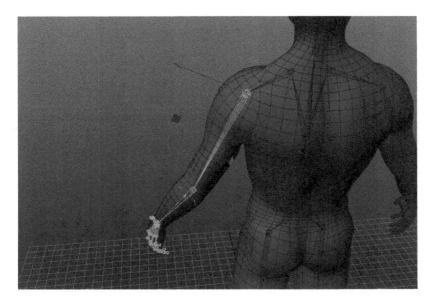

FIGURE 5.7 **(See color insert.)** The Humerus of this model nicely conforms to
the Y, X, +X Joint Orient options.

FIGURE 5.8 **(See color insert.)** The elbow has an incorrect alignment with the Y, X, +X Orient Options—its rotate plane on the X-axis isn't really aligned with its natural hinge axis.

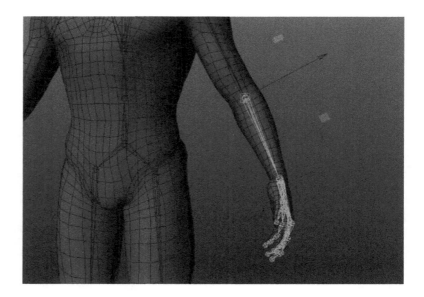

FIGURE 5.9 **(See color insert.)** Changing to the Y, X, +Z Joint Orient options will fix the orientation of the elbow. Now its Z-axis will be the main axis of rotation, which is different from the shoulder, but as long as it conforms to the Y-down guideline it doesn't really matter.

5.2 WHEN DO I NEED TO CUSTOMIZE MY JOINT ORIENTS? HOW DO I SET CUSTOM JOINT ORIENTS?

Custom Joint Orient values become necessary when we are setting up areas that don't easily conform to the world alignment. This is *especially* true in the fingers and thumb joints, since in a relaxed pose they have all kinds of odd alignments. Often the rigger will have to custom-orient these joints in order to have them rotate properly. Let's look at the index finger of our model to see how this works. As you can see in Figure 5.10, the index finger joints have been placed and parented as close to the model's anatomy as possible while maintaining their individual alignments. Yet they are all still set to the World axis orientation. Now we must orient them, individually or all at once, in order to create the bending action of the finger. The knuckles are all hinge joints, which means that all of them will be bending on the X-Axis as the main axis, and the upper knuckle also has the ability to rotate on the Z-axis (using the Y-down guideline).

Now when I try to orient the finger joints, I get a problem. None of my options will give me the exact results I am looking for! The reason for this is that the finger is so offline with the world axes that there's no way to get the cardinal axis information to the joints in a way that works for this

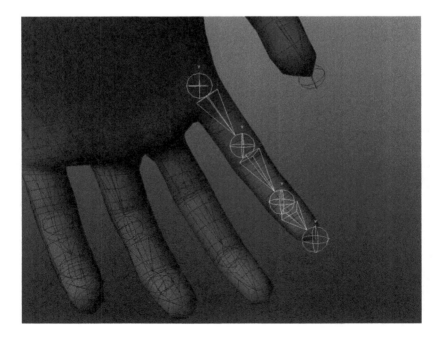

FIGURE 5.10   The Index finger chain positioned and parented but not oriented.

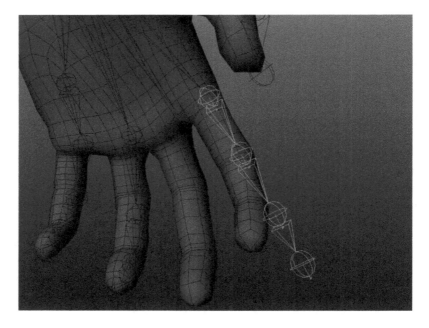

FIGURE 5.11 The finger joint, with all the knuckle joints (except the top) straightened by setting the joint orient values to zero.

alignment, as you can see in Figure 5.11. The best way to deal with this problem is to *zero* out all of the joint orients of the knuckle joints, making sure that they are completely straight, and then "bend" them into place using the joint orient values that we exposed in the Channel Box. This will ensure that you get a well-aligned finger joint.

Keep in mind that good results for this type of manual orientation of a joint can be difficult to achieve, but without doing this you will never have proper alignment and hence the proper bending of the joints in question. The fingers of a character model are particularly tricky, so always pay careful attention to setting them properly! It is almost a universal problem that the model will not be perfectly aligned with all the knuckles, so you might have to do a little creative orienting in order to get it right (Figures 5.12 and 5.13).

The thumb, as you can see in Figures 5.14 and 5.15, is another problem area. You will need an "extra" joint to generate the hinging effect of the thumb, which makes it opposable to the rest of the hand. In order to get this orientation right, you must make it possible to fold the thumb across the palm of the hand from the base, like it is in Figure 5.16. Once again, creative joint orients are really important here—make sure that the action of the thumb is correct!

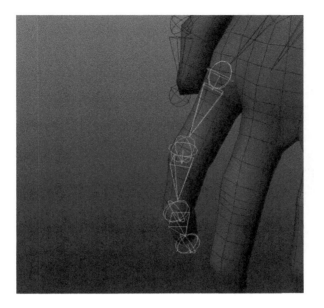

FIGURE 5.12   The fingers, oriented into place properly instead of rotated into place.

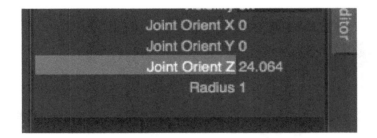

FIGURE 5.13   Editing the Joint orient value directly. This can be dangerous, but we try to constrain it to only one axis while the others remain zero.

5.3 WHAT ARE TWIST NODES? HOW DO I PUT TWIST NODES INTO MY SKELETON?

Twist nodes are joints that exist in-between primary skeletal joints that use the spindle or "twist" axis to offset it from other joints for deformation purposes. Our first spine joint we created in the last chapter is a twist joint, in that it does not represent a solid mass or actual skeletal joint, but is there as a "helper" joint, for deformation purposes. Certain parts of the human body, especially our arms, have tremendous amount of twisty flexibility, which is very hard to reproduce with the basic skeleton alone. We need to add these to our human skeleton for proper deformation.

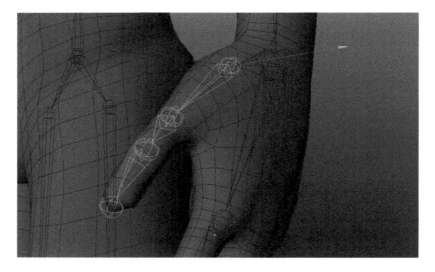

FIGURE 5.14 The thumb "extra" joint, which is what makes it opposable and a pain to set up for proper rotation.

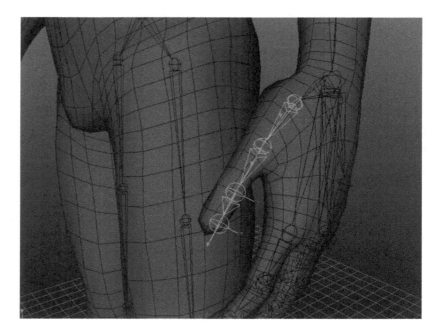

FIGURE 5.15 The thumb being set up for proper customized orientation.

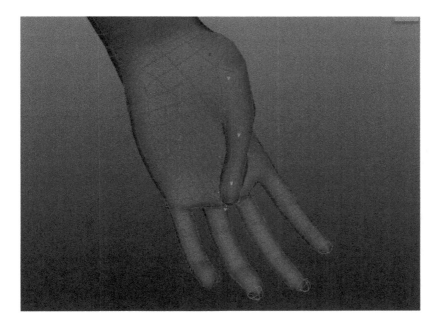

FIGURE 5.16 The opposable action of the thumb. Sometimes this requires a lot of finesse to get it right!

5.4 WHAT TWIST NODES DO I NEED TO CREATE FOR MY HUMAN SKELETON?

Technically you don't need *any* twist nodes for a proper motion skeleton, and indeed motion capture has a very hard time detecting certain types of twists in a character's limbs—they're generally inferred by the positional data. *But*, if you want a character to deform properly and *look* good with a mesh bound to it, you're going to need some way of dealing with the twisting action of the spine, legs, and arms.

We've already created the spine joint we need, so that one is taken care of! But now we really need to look at the twisting action of the arm. The problem with the arm is that we can twist it in two areas—both the forearm *and* the Humerus twist. The Humerus twists because it's a ball and socket joint and freely rotating in three planes is essential to its nature. But the twisting action of the upper arm in terms of deformation can cause all kinds of problems in this area, which we will cover in Chapter 9. It's not essential, however, in creating the basic all-purpose character rig for animation, so we will skip it for now.

The forearm is a different matter. While it may seem like the wrist itself twists on the Y-axis (or whatever your spindle axis is), in truth we have two forearm bones, called the Ulna and Radius, and they spin around one another, like a towel wringing out, which gives you the ability to give somebody a "thumbs up" or a "thumbs down." You have almost more than 200 degrees of freedom in the spin axis with your Humerus and forearm combined! The problem is that, for various reasons, we need another joint in the forearm in order to create the effect of the ulna and radius, one of the main ones being the deformation problem. We can't rotate the wrist in its spin axis or it will look broken and we certainly can't spin the elbow! The solution is to create *another* joint, in-between the elbow and the wrist.

5.5 HOW DO I INSERT A TWIST JOINT IF I NEED ONE?

In order to insert a joint in-between two joints in a hierarchy while preserving the hierarchy, we need to unparent the child joint (in this case the wrist) first. Then we duplicate the elbow, name it forearm, and parent it to the elbow (since it was duplicated from the elbow it would have been parented to the Humerus as a sibling). *Now* we just translate it along the Primary axis in local space (we are using Y as the primary) and it will follow the original joint orient perfectly as we put it in the middle, then parent the wrist to it. This is the long way—in Maya there's an "Insert Joint Tool" that does all this work for you automatically, if you're using Maya and want to save time. It wasn't always so, however, and sadly us old-time riggers used to do this operation by hand often (Figures 5.17 through 5.19).

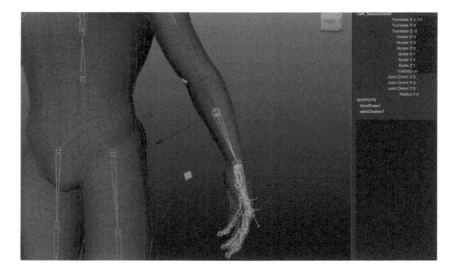

FIGURE 5.17 Behold the forearm twist node perfectly aligned to the elbow and wrist. Notice it has zero values for its joint orients!

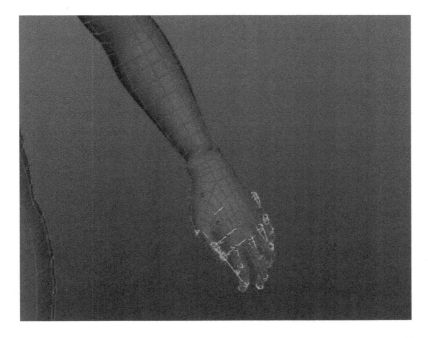

FIGURE 5.18   The result of twisting the wrist joint without using a twist node.

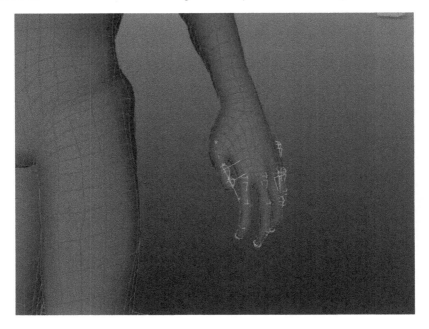

FIGURE 5.19   Much better! The twist node, instead of the wrist joint, is being rotated. It still needs some work, but it doesn't look "broken" anymore.

Although a single twist node will vastly improve your results in terms of deformation, most serious professional rigs use three to four joints for twisting, which provides a much smoother result. Also, the more complex rigs do this for the tibia (calf area) as well, which makes the legs more flexible but adds more levels of complexity. This book is about the *essential* elements of a character rig. You can't do without arm rotation; it's essential to human movement. The legs are much less flexible, and hence we don't always need this extra stuff. But if you want to put it in there, use the same methodology as we did for the arms. In Lesson 5 in this book, you will find a much more detailed set of instructions for creating, setting, and driving twist nodes.

5.6 DO I HAVE TO DO ALL THIS ON THE OTHER SIDE?

Heck no! If there's one thing computers are good at, it's repeating complex tasks in the same order. All we have to do is to use the Mirror Joints action across the YZ plane using "Behavior" as an option (in Maya) and we have a perfect mirror of the limb (remember to do this to the top limb in the chain, in this case the Clavicle). And now you've done it! The basic skeleton, oriented and inserted twist nodes, is now ready for the next step (Figure 5.20).

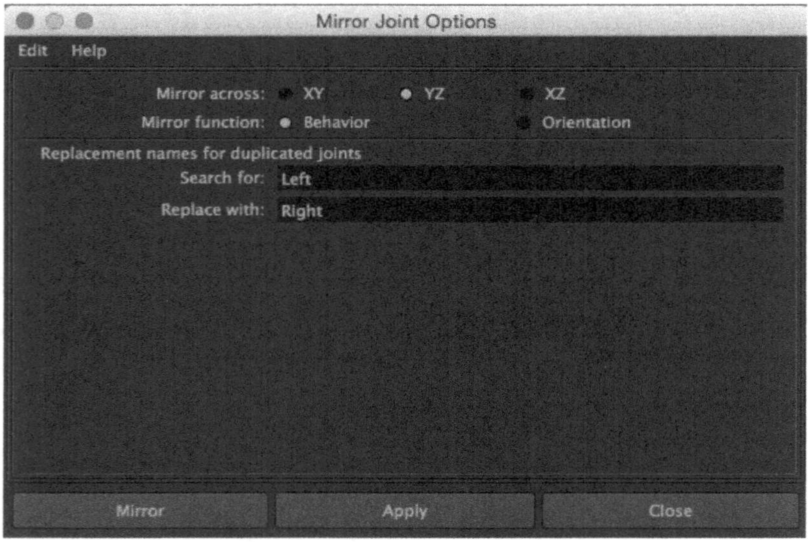

FIGURE 5.20 Mirroring the joint chains from one side to another. The behavior option will flip the Joint Orients, while the orientation option will not.

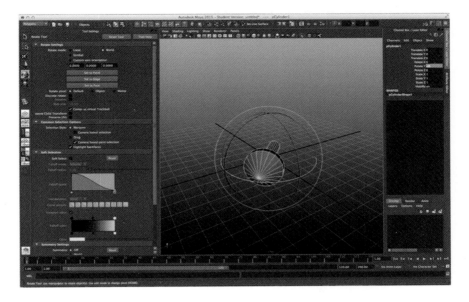

FIGURE 2.3 World rotation coordinates have the same orientation no matter what the rotation channels of x, y, and z are.

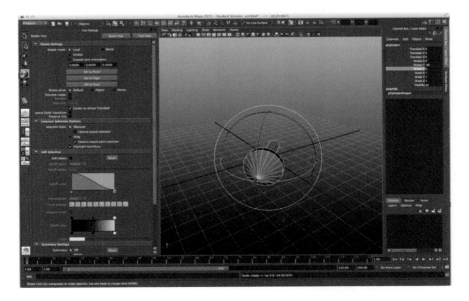

FIGURE 2.4 The local rotation coordinate space aligns all the circles with the direction the arrow is pointing, which is convenient for rotating in specific directions, but is actually an illusion.

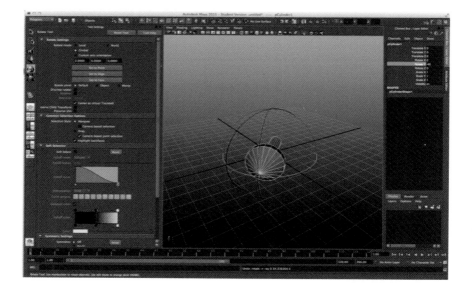

FIGURE 2.5 Using the gimbal rotational coordinate system, the X-axis has changed its alignment to match the direction of the arrow, but the Z has remained the same.

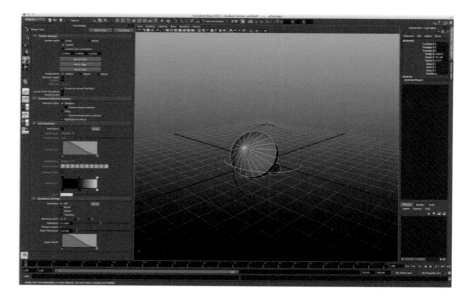

FIGURE 2.6 Gimbal lock occurs when one of these semi-independent circles crosses another axis, such as the X-axis and Z-axis are about to in this image.

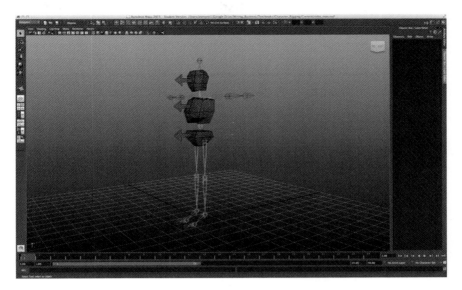

FIGURE 4.7　The major planes of the human vertical axis.

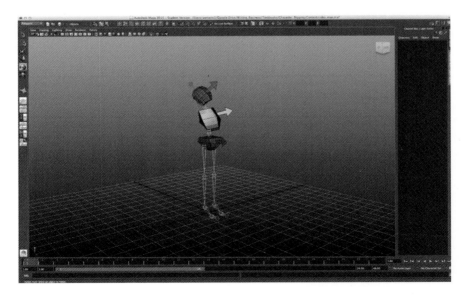

FIGURE 4.8　These planes can be pointing in multiple directions due to the flexibility of the spine.

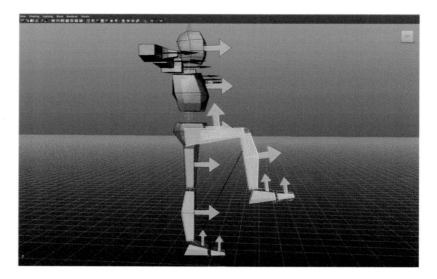

FIGURE 4.9 The hip is the fulcrum of the upper leg, which rotates the furthest range of motion toward your belly.

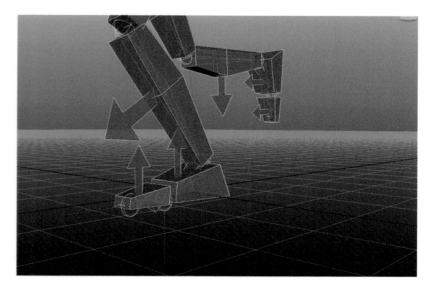

FIGURE 4.10 The planes of orientation related to the foot and ankle when the foot is planted on the ground.

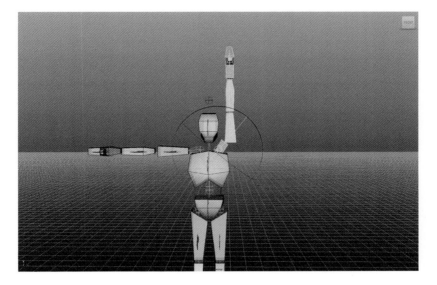

FIGURE 4.11   Lifting the arms above the head requires the Clavicle to rotate in the World Z-axis here.

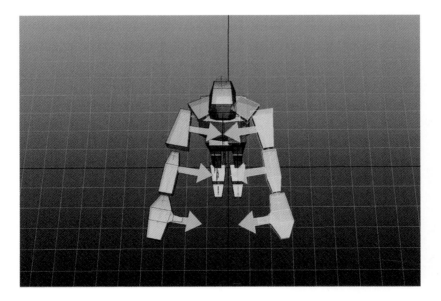

FIGURE 4.12   The hinging of the Clavicle forward.

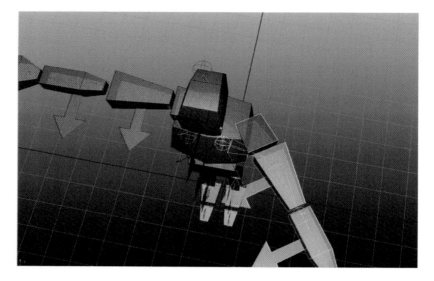

FIGURE 4.13   Don't let the Clavicle node be too far in front of the body midaxis, like it is here.

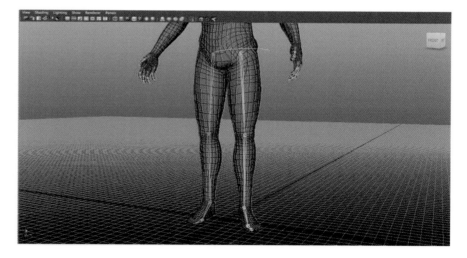

FIGURE 4.23   The twisting of the leg from the Femur.

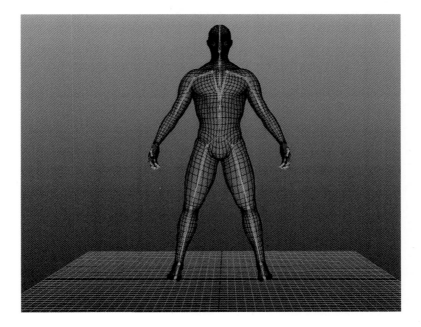

FIGURE 5.3 Legs are wide, but ankles are aligned with the leg.

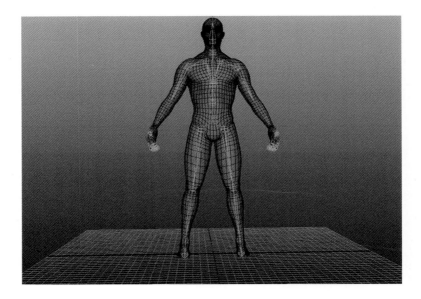

FIGURE 5.4 Legs are wide, but the feet are firmly planted on the ground. This means the ankle, ball, and toe are good to go with World Axis alignments as they are—no orients needed.

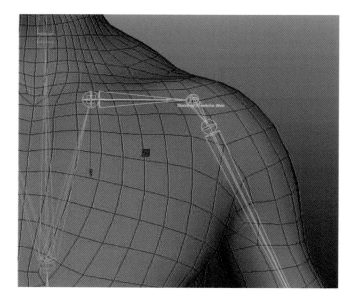

FIGURE 5.6   The "dummy" joint preserving the basic alignment of the Clavicle while adhering to the Y-down-the-bone guideline. It's only necessary if you have a pipeline which requires it; otherwise just leave the Clavicle oriented to the world.

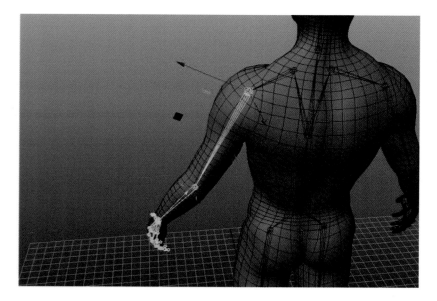

FIGURE 5.7   The Humerus of this model nicely conforms to the Y, X, +X Joint Orient options.

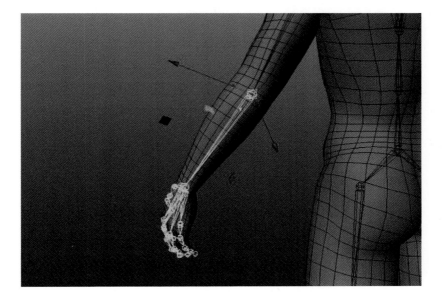

FIGURE 5.8 The elbow has an incorrect alignment with the Y, X, +X Orient Options—its rotate plane on the X-axis isn't really aligned with its natural hinge axis.

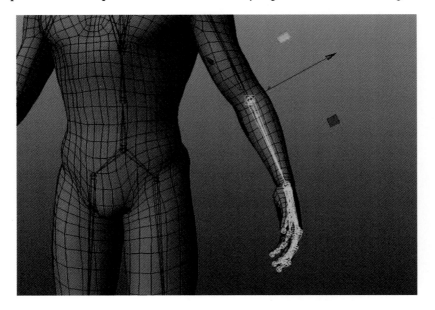

FIGURE 5.9 Changing to the Y, X, +Z Joint Orient options will fix the orientation of the elbow. Now its Z-axis will be the main axis of rotation, which is different from the shoulder, but as long as it conforms to the Y-down guideline it doesn't really matter.

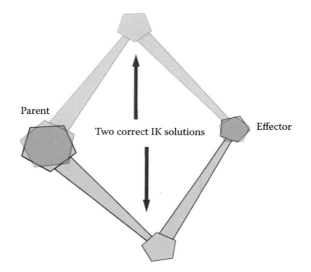

FIGURE 6.1 Two possible rotational IK solutions based on the position of the child or effector joint.

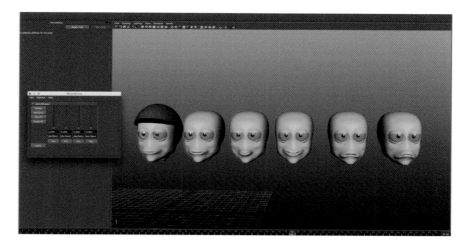

FIGURE 7.7 Blend shape targets for a cartoon head, lined up in a row. The shape on the far left is the Base Shape and all the rest are targets that the base shape will "morph" to when the slider values are adjusted (character head model by artist Fred Mathis).

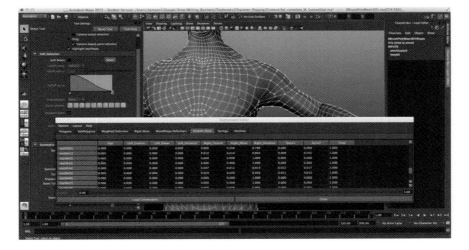

FIGURE 8.1 The Component Editor showing all of the details about the selected vertices and the skin weight values listed for each joint.

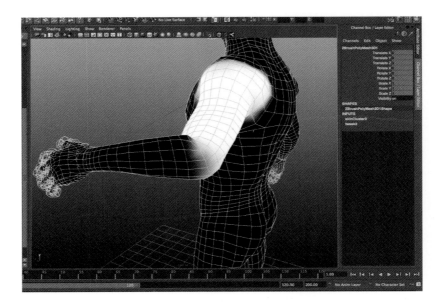

FIGURE 8.2 The light and dark areas of an Artisan toolset allowing the artist to paint joint influences organically.

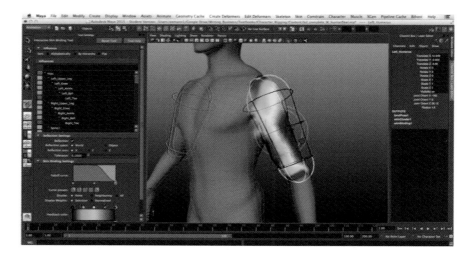

FIGURE 8.3 The Interactive Binding method, which has capsules that use volume influence to control how much influence a joint has over the vertices inside it.

FIGURE 8.5 The Artisan Interface for skinning weights on a smooth bound character.

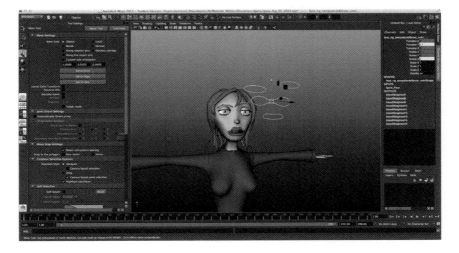

FIGURE 9.1   The floating curves are used to control the many parts of the face joints.

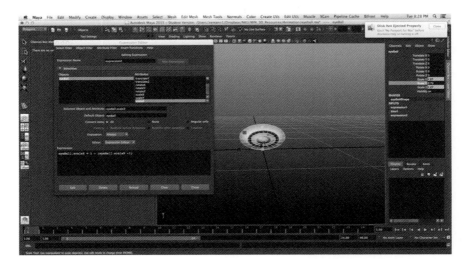

FIGURE 9.7   The squishy ball, now automated with an expression. I guess we have to do some math after all.

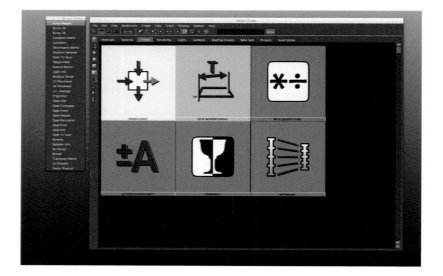

FIGURE 9.8 Some math utility nodes that are frequently useful in character rigging.

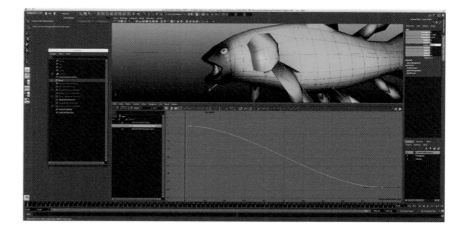

FIGURE 9.10 The relationship of a driven key animation curve. The fish jaw opening is controlled by the interpolation of the values between the keys of the attribute slider.

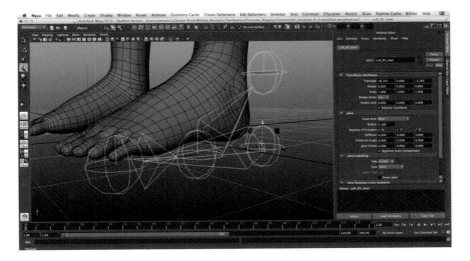

FIGURE 9.13 This is the reverse foot skeleton. Notice that it's not a part of the base skeleton. It's a whole separate thing that is used as a rigging element. Also notice that it has been moved slightly off to the side so that it is visible. Normally, it would be right on top of the regular foot joints.

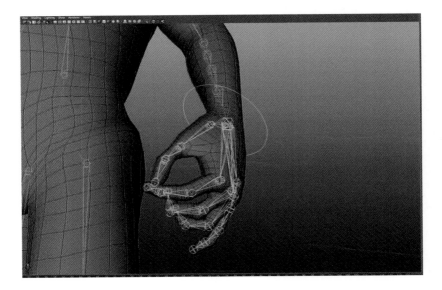

FIGURE 9.23 The articulated hand joints. The NURBS Circle is the rigging node we'll be using to control the arm limb.

FIGURE 9.46 Make sure that the lock toggle button is in the off state for the newly added joints.

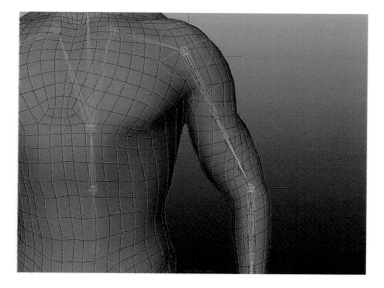

FIGURE 9.50 It was a lot of work, but look at the end result! Much better than Figure 9.38!

CHAPTER 6

Inverse Kinematics

6.1 WHAT IS INVERSE KINEMATICS?

Kinematics is an interesting word. It means the science of geometry of motion, and indeed it's vital in determining how things move both in the real world and in the 3D world, where we are trying to mimic that real world as best we can. In Chapters 1 and 2 we learned about hierarchies and joints. We touched on Kinematics briefly, in the sense that it is when the rotation of the Parent controls the translation of the Child object in an arc around that parent's pivot. This, as we learned, is known as *Forward Kinematics* or *FK* for short.

Forward kinematics is how your body would move if it were free-floating in space or mostly how we move when we are swimming. That is to say, your brain sends electric impulses to your muscles, which twitch on command, pulling your tendons and ligaments so that the skeletal joints rotate in the direction you intend. All of this happens at near the speed of light, often times completely instinctively! So if you are standing there, your left arm swinging by your side (your right arm, I assume, is holding this book), you can flex your bicep and raise your arm to 90°. Your wrist, being connected, moves with the elbow and now you can see that the wrist is moving in an arc around the elbow. If we had our character handy, we could do something similar in our 3D program—rotate the elbow, watch the elbow rotate on its hinge axis, and the wrist going along with it. Seems pretty simple, right?

Let's add some complexity. Now imagine you have a friend, who grabs your wrist and pulls it. What happens? Well, unless you are Mr. Fantastic or Gumby, your elbow and possibly Humerus *rotate* to accommodate the position of the wrist. Hey, wait a second, you might ask, how come now all of the sudden the parent joints are *rotating* based on the *translation* of my wrist? Well, my friend, you have just stumbled upon what we in the world of 3D character rigging call *Inverse Kinematics*, or *IK*. Whenever a force is applied to the position of one of your joints, like your friend pulling your wrist, or the ground applying force to your feet, it's using *inverse* kinematics. The forward kinematic equation of parent rotation causing the child to translate can be *inverted* and we can start rotating the parent based on the position of the child. We know what the rotation of the parent should be, since the child must always be the same distance from the pivot. With just two joints and only one plane of rotation, this is pretty easy to figure out—there are only two solutions! Figure 6.1 shows both possibilities of solutions to the adjusted position of the child joint.

Inverse kinematics is a system comprised of several components. The *Effector* is the actual point in space from which the position is derived. We don't use the actual child joint itself, since its translation is really controlled by the rotation of its parent. We're just using a position in space, derived from the effector, to tell the other joints how to rotate. The *IK Handle* is the object that you select in 3D space (using Maya), and the *IK Solver* is the mathematical expression that calculates the rotations, based on internal

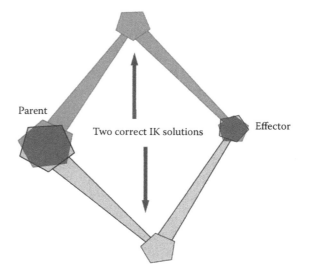

Parent

Two correct IK solutions

Effector

FIGURE 6.1 **(See color insert.)** Two possible rotational IK solutions based on the position of the child or effector joint.

math and several input attributes on the individual joints in the chain. You translate the IK handle in space and the Effector moves with it, which in turn will feed into the IK Solver calculation and rotate the joints to match it.

Now, getting this to work for two joints in a chain is also possible, but, of course, more complex. When we have three joints in a chain, just like our Humerus, elbow, and wrist, there are several combinations of rotations that could be correct for any given position of the effector. In the real world, this is all controlled by the physical limitations of the human body. Your elbow only bends in one plane since it's a hinge joint, and even then only from 0° (arm extended) to about 120°, (fully closed) so the possible combinations are limited. Your Humerus is a ball-and-socket joint, which means it has 3 degrees of rotation and must be free to use all of them to adjust to this inverse relationship. Remember all those weird attributes only joints possess? Well, now we can use them in order to limit our IK solver possibilities (more on this later).

6.2 WHY DO I NEED INVERSE KINEMATICS?

Now that we know what IK is, why we need it is an excellent question! Many times animators and riggers jump all over IK before really investigating just what they need it for, and why it would be beneficial in some way. IK is excellent for re-creating the situation in which a character is not moving his or her limbs of their own volition or when they are locked onto or being pulled by a force other than themselves. So if your character is swimming or flying, it doesn't really *need* IK for any specific reason. Most of these free-floating animations can be done well with forward kinematics (which we'll call FK from now on). FK gives us plenty of freedom to animate without some of the unpredictable results of IK. But where IK really shines, however, is in doing things that FK can't or at least not without a lot of effort.

IK is great for places where we *need* the position of the limb to stay put, but have the rest of the body rotate around it. This is best evidenced by the feet! The feet always stay in one place when planted on the ground, and any time you move your body with your feet planted on the ground, the body will move *around* the pivot of the ankle, ball, or heel of that foot. So in 3D, when we want to have a character walking, it's really difficult to use FK to generate an animation for that foot. But it's a breeze with IK. In Figure 6.2, you can see how the feet have stayed planted on the ground when the root joint of our character has been translated in the Y-axis. In Figure 6.3, you can see the same Y-axis value, but this time without IK!

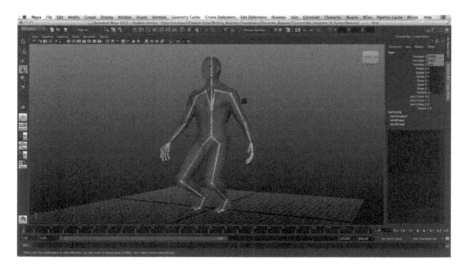

FIGURE 6.2   The Hips, translated on the Y-axis, with IK on. Notice how the knees and ankles bend to match a natural position? Pretty cool, huh?

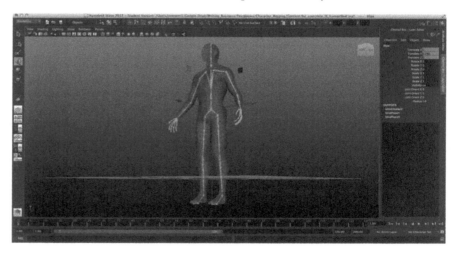

FIGURE 6.3   The Hips, translated the same amount on the Y-axis, without IK. Not very cool at all. The feet just move through the ground plane.

Another nice thing about IK and why it is used in areas other than the feet is that it is much easier to generate animation data using a single object's translation in space than it is trying to keep track of keyframed rotations on three or more joints! You only have one thing to worry about (more or less). For this reason, it is used in the creation of animations for the arms, *despite the fact that most arm animation is generated by way of personal volition instead of forces acting upon them.* This is an important distinction to make for a lot of reasons. IK can be very helpful for arm animation, but it can be just as detrimental as well (as we will see in a bit). Sometimes animating an arm action on a character can be much easier with FK.

6.3 HOW DO I CREATE IK CHAINS?

IK chains are created by using the IK Handle Tool in Maya, then picking the beginning and end of the chain desired. One thing to note here is that, any joint inside the chain (but not including the effector joint in the chain) has its rotations entirely controlled by the IK solver. This means you can't independently rotate them. You can have as many joints in an IK chain as you want, but the more joints you have, the more possible rotational solution you will have, and hence the less predictable it will become. Most of the IK chains we will be using will have only three joints in the chain—which we want to set up for the Humerus–elbow–wrist chain, and the Femur–knee–ankle chain. We will also want to create two-joint IK chains from the ankle to the ball and the ball to the toe joints, in order to "lock down" the feet. Specific creation of IK chains for the basic human will be discussed in finer detail in the lesson for this chapter.

6.4 WHAT'S THE DIFFERENCE BETWEEN SINGLE-CHAIN AND ROTATE-PLANE IK? WHAT IS A POLE VECTOR?

IK solvers in Maya, and most 3D packages, come in two primary types: single chain and rotate plane. The difference between these two types is based on the Pole Vector and how it is controlled. A Pole Vector is the amount of "twisting" that occurs in the action of the IK chain or more specifically the plane of rotation upon which the solver is working for. But this is very confusing based on the definition. Instead of worrying about all that math stuff, let's try an experiment. I want you to hold your hands out at chest height, just like in Figure 6.4. Now without moving your wrist *position*, go ahead and "swing" your elbows down like in Figure 6.5.

Because IK has more than one solution for any given position of the end effector (in this case the wrist), both of these arm rotation configurations are correct to the IK solver! But which one do you want? The answer to this is dependent on your animation, *but* it's really important to get the right one, isn't it? The way we control this is with the Pole Vector, which essentially controls the amount of twisting that will occur at the top of the IK chain in order to point the middle joint in the direction we want it to go.

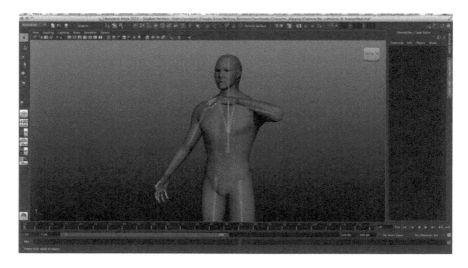

FIGURE 6.4   One way to hold your hands at chest height.

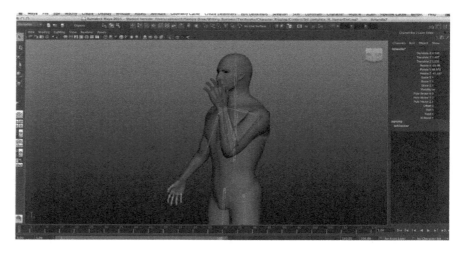

FIGURE 6.5   Your wrists are in the same position in space, but the arms are in a totally different configuration!

When we choose Single-Chain solver or Rotate-Plane solver, we are choosing the method with which we can use to control this action.

A Single-Chain IK solver will change this when the IK handle itself is rotated, which means that when you rotate the IK handle, the Pole Vector will rotate as well, twisting the arm to match your intended rotation plane. The nice thing about this is that it's simpler; you just have to animate both the translation and rotation of the IK handle. The bad thing about this is that it's kind of unpredictable because the orientation of an IK handle realigns itself with the joint hierarchy, which means that Euler rotations can be tricky with animated data in this regard, resulting in unpredictable behavior.

The Rotate-Plane IK solver uses a Pole Vector, which is a point in space that the IK handle aims at in order to keep itself stable. This technique uses a position value instead of a rotation value, usually in the form of a Pole Vector Constraint, which is far more stable to animate. This also means that rotating an RP solver IK handle will not change the rotations of the joints at all. The nice thing about this setup is that it's far more stable and predictable, but the down side is that it's harder to set up and you have two objects instead of one to manage (the pole vector constraint object and the IK handle).

One thing we can discuss here is the advantage/disadvantage ratio not only of single-chain vs. rotate-plane IK solvers for the arms, but also of the usefulness of IK on the arms *period*. As any experienced animator can tell you, trying to monkey around with the pole vector and animate it on top of the IK handle control can be a royal pain and end up causing you to spend more time trying to *fix* the animation than actually make it look *good*. Most modern rigging solutions have a simple toggle to swap IK and FK methods for animation, making it a one-stop solution for animators, giving them the freedom to choose. This is the best solution because many of your animations for the arms won't really require IK in the first place if your characters hand isn't planted on the ground or set up in some way that would require it to be planted while the rest of the body moves around it. The legs, on the other hand, really benefit from IK since they spend a lot of time being planted on the ground. There is no one single solution that works for everything—most rigs are either very generalized or very specific.

The feet, just to clarify, are set up a certain way with those extra, two-joint IK chains from the ankle to the ball and the ball to the toe, in order to lock down those joints to the ground in a setup we call the Rolling Foot, which allows the ankle to rotate and flex from its own pivot and also rotate around the ball when the heel lifts up off of the ground. The specific setup for the foot will be addressed in the lesson for this chapter.

6.5 HOW DO I EDIT IK CHAINS AND THEIR PARAMETERS?

Remember in Chapter 2, when we looked over all those joint-specific attributes? Well, now we get to see how they actually work. The degrees of freedom of any particular joint tell our IK solver exactly which plane the joint can rotate on. In Figure 6.6, you can see the settings for the elbow, which

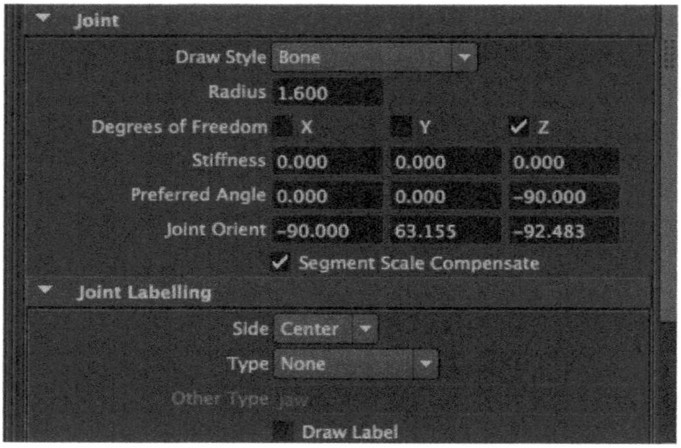

FIGURE 6.6   The settings for the elbow, limiting it to only one plane of rotation.

has been allowed only the freedom to rotate on the Euler Z-axis. If we don't limit the hinge joint to the proper rotation plane it could rotate any way it pleases, as long as it worked for the solver. Limiting it to one rotation plane will force it to only act in a single vector, just like in real life. If you don't set this for the hinge joints, which are usually the joints in the middle of the chain, you can get unpredictable results (Figure 6.7)! One important note here is that you want to keep all three channels of rotation free for the parent joint in the chain (the Humerus in this case) because otherwise it can lead to unpredictable and highly unstable results.

The other three important parameters are stiffness, rotational damping, and preferred angle. "Stiffness" is the likelihood of a joint rotating inside an IK chain. It is used when you want certain joints in the chain to rotate more easily than others. This is not something we use a lot in human-based IK, since our chains are pretty straightforward and limited to three joints. It's of much greater use when you have an IK chain with four or more joints and some are more flexible than others, like in a tail or tentacle.

"Rotational damping" is a setting that creates a movement "dampening" effect, where the rotation of a joint gets stiffer the closer it gets to a maximum rotational point. This is pretty advanced stuff, but not such a terrible idea to tweak because the compression of kinetic energy is not linear—as you reach the end of the elbow's rotation, for instance, it will require more energy to "squeeze" into the final position. But this is a thing we can re-create in the animation curves as well (and in a much more

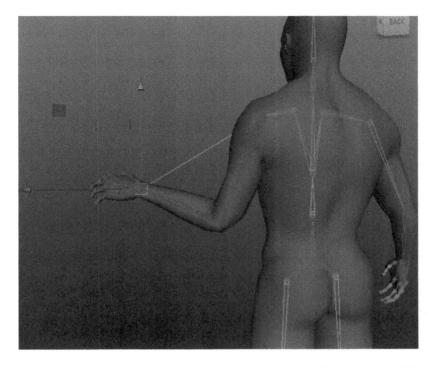

FIGURE 6.7 Moving the IK handle without setting the elbow degrees of freedom. Looks painful!

predictable manner). I only use these settings for very specific rigs that can benefit from it, like say a tail for a scorpion.

"Preferred angle" is another attribute that controls the way IK chains solve, and it tells the joint which direction it "prefers" to move, or which solution is the correct one, given two or more options. If you look again at Figure 6.1, you can see that there are two correct solutions to the same position of the child joint—the preferred angle of rotation of a joint will give the solver a clue into which one you would prefer is correct. If you have a joint IK chain that is a straight line it will often not bend the middle joint if these values are zero, because the solver won't know which way to rotate the chain!

One thing that is important to note is the fact that *all* of the parameters just discussed here, that is, stiffness, damping, and preferred angle, including the type of IK solver, should *always* be set *before* creating the IK chain. The results of changing these after creating the IK chain are usually completely unpredictable. I usually have to tweak the values and re-create the IK chains several times during the development of a rig.

6.6 WHAT ARE THE IK ESSENTIALS FOR THE HUMANOID BODY?

The human body needs two IK setups in order to function properly—we can add as many as we want but in the spirit of keeping things as simple as possible we really only need to set up the Humerus to the forearm/wrist, the Femur to the ankle, and the ankle–ball–toe (called the rolling foot). Anything else is superfluous and unnecessary (although very useful for certain things). The arms, when using IK, almost always *need* those IK handles to be rotate-plane solvers, so that the elbow can be aimed or pointed in the right plane of rotation. The legs are generally set up the same way, but I generally argue that unless your character is Spider-Man, some wicked martial artist, or a ballerina, the range of motion on the legs is going to be limited enough to where you don't really need the rotate-plane setup or the twist nodes. But hey—this is 3D animation! Our characters are *always* comic-book heroes or supervillains or ballerinas! So most general purpose rigs are made with flexibility in mind, and they tend to use Rotate-Plane IK setups for the legs as well as the arms.

6.7 WHAT IS SPLINE IK?

"Spline IK" is worth a mention here because it's an IK form that has multiple uses—just not in humans! It's really useful for creating something like an octopus tentacle, a chain swinging, or a long animal tail. Spline IK uses a joint chain and a NURBS curve to control the rotation of the joints. Basically, wherever the curve goes, so do the joints in turn. If you move the CV points on the curve, the joints will rotate to match the direction of the path, which is the straight line between points in the curve. Another feature of Spline IK is that the joints will only translate *along* the curve, which makes it a very unique way of generating deformation along an arc for things like muscles of the face, which move very specifically (Figure 6.8).

Inverse Kinematics is a very handy tool, as you've seen here in this brief introduction. There are many, many deeper levels to IK and its uses, but because we want to concentrate on the essentials of human-based rigging, I am limiting this chapter to what you need to know in order to set up an all-purpose rig. Now that you understand the fundamental concepts, you can take it in any direction you want. More specifics are discussed in the lessons for this chapter, in which we set up the basic IK structure as discussed in this chapter and also the Reverse Foot Setup, a way to get the most out of your foot controls for your character. IK is a mysterious entity at first, but it quickly becomes more familiar with use. Both pitfalls and

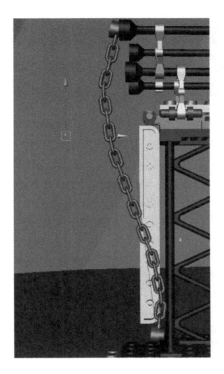

FIGURE 6.8   A chain swinging; set up with a Spline IK solver. Spline IK is useful for things such as this.

advantages of its use become clearer as you encounter and solve specific problems with it. My best advice in this arena is to go with the simplest solution for what you need first before you begin to construct complex IK rigs—things can get very frustrating, very quickly!

6.8 LESSON 1: BUILDING STANDARD IK CHAINS FOR A HUMAN ARM

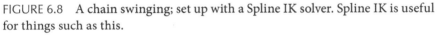

In order to learn the basic aspects of IK, we are going to build the IK chains for the arm of a human. In the standard setup, we build an IK chain from the Humerus to the first twist node of the forearm (if there is a twist node) and then set the effector to operate from the position of the wrist joint. Doing this is key in freeing the forearm to twist from the middle, and not from the wrist joint, which will result in a "broken" wrist appearance due to the mechanics of the skin cluster. The human forearm does not really twist from the wrist, but instead it relies on two joints in the forearm called the ulna and radius, as you can see in Figure 6.9.

FIGURE 6.9 The human forearm. These two joints roll around and wring like a towel in order to roll the wrist.

Even though the real-life mechanism for rolling the forearm has two bones, we don't really have to construct it this way—we can just add a joint in-between the elbow and wrist to take care of it. Generally speaking, for deformation purposes we would really want at *least* two joints for this, and ideally four, but for the sake of simplification I will be using just one here. In the video series accompanying the book, I'll go over how to drive the four-joint setup that I generally use (Figure 6.10).

Now, before we create the IK chain, it's a good idea to set our joint's IK preferences in the Attribute Editor. Changing this *after* creating the chain can often cause unexpected results. Select the elbow and open up the Attribute Editor. Make sure that the joint in question has its degrees of freedom set to the exact plane it should be rotating on, and no other axis. Below are the parameters I set for the arm joints (based on the previous joint orients):

FIGURE 6.10 The single forearm twist joint in-between the elbow and wrist.

The Humerus should be left free to rotate on all three axes. This is vital in order for the IK to work properly.

The Elbow should be limited to only the Z-axis and have a preferred angle of −90° in that axis. This makes it hinge in only one direction, just like an elbow should.

The Forearm Twist joint should only rotate in the Y-axis. Preferred angle is not necessary here, since it will be a twist node only.

The Wrist should be able to rotate in only the X and Z axes, but not the Y (Figure 6.11).

Now that the IK preferences are set, we can create the IK handle and edit it. Go to Skeleton > IK Handle Tool (Figure 6.12) and open the options box, which will bring up the tool settings. We are going to use the Rotate Plane IK Solver, which offers us the ability to set a Pole Vector, which controls the plane upon which the solver operates and changes the way the elbow points when the arm is being solved. The IK Handle Tool, since it is a Tool, requires you to choose the beginning (parent) and the end (child) of the chain. Here we are going to select first the Humerus and then the Forearm Twist (not the Wrist!). We need the Forearm Twist and the Wrist node to be free to twist and rotate independently (Figures 6.13 and 6.14).

FIGURE 6.11 Joint IK Preferences for the elbow. Notice how I have set the degrees of freedom to only the Z-axis and the preferred angle to −90, which will ensure that the elbow rotates as it should, and only as it should.

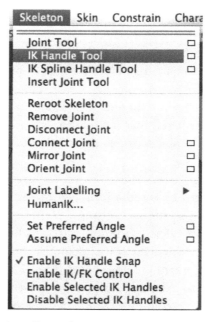

FIGURE 6.12   The IK Handle Tool command.

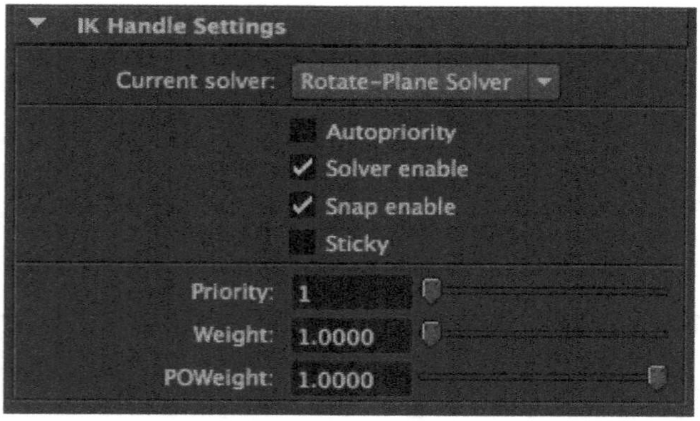

FIGURE 6.13   The IK Handle Tool Options. For the shoulder and hips, we always use a Rotate-Plane IK solver.

The next step here is to change the initial position of the IK handle to the Wrist joint. In order to do so, we need to do a little trick where we change the pivot of the Effector. Select the IK handle and open the Window > Hypergraph > Connections (Figures 6.15 and 6.16).

Select the Effector in the Hypergraph and then enter pivot mode by hitting the Insert key on a PC or the fn–left arrow keys on a Mac. This will allow you to change the pivot of the Effector to the Wrist joint, as you can see in Figure 6.17.

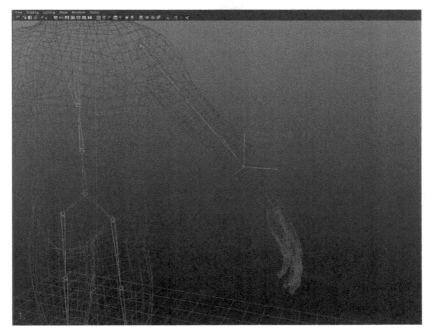

FIGURE 6.14 The IK Handle has been created between the Humerus and the Forearm twist.

Window	Assets	Animate	Geometr
General Editors		▶	
Rendering Editors		▶	
Animation Editors		▶	
Relationship Editors		▶	
Settings/Preferences		▶	
Attribute Editor			
Outliner		O	
Node Editor			
Create Node			
Hypergraph: Hierarchy		☐	
Hypergraph: Connections		☐	
Paint Effects			
UV Texture Editor			
Playblast		☐	
View Arrangement		▶	
Saved Layouts		▶	
Save Current Layout...			
Frame All in All Views		⇧A	
Frame Selection in All Views		⇧F	
Raise Main Window			
Raise Application Windows			

FIGURE 6.15 Open the Hypergraph Connections.

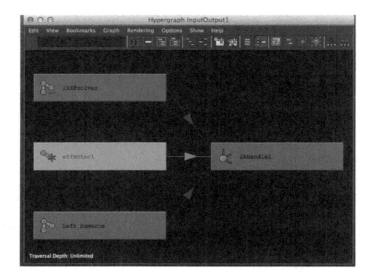

FIGURE 6.16   The input graph of the IK handle. Select the Effector connected to it.

FIGURE 6.17   The pivot of the Effector is now at the Wrist, which will move the IK Handle's initial position there as well.

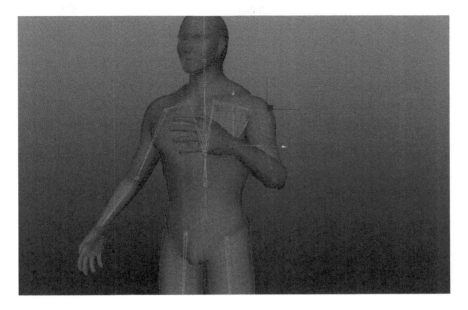

FIGURE 6.18 The IK handle in action.

Now we have an IK solution for the arm that allows us to freely move the arm with the IK handle, but leaves the forearm twist and the wrist free to rotate independently. One thing to note is that this is the *simplest* forearm/wrist IK setup we can use. In the final lessons of this book, you will find a much more complex solution for the forearm twist that yields far smoother and more accurate results (Figure 6.18).

II

Deformation

CHAPTER 7

Introduction to Deformation

7.1 WHAT IS A DEFORMER? HOW DO DEFORMERS WORK?

So what exactly *is* deformation? Up until now, we've been talking about 3D rotations, joints, hierarchies, and kinematics. This has all been about *rotation*. Now we are entering into the second important phase of character rigging: deformation. It's a lot harder to define than rotation! Deformation is the adjustment of geometry in a proportional manner based on some kind of external object or action. What happens is that the geometry (in the form of vertices or NURBS CVs) is *offset* from its original position while maintaining proportional relationships to all the other vertices in the object. These offsets are maintained in some mathematical formula by the deformer node, which is actually something that exists as a piece of the history stack. When you deform something, you preserve the original shape of the vertices, but apply offsets to them based on the nature of the deformer. Different deformers have different ways of displacing the vertices.

7.2 WHAT ARE THE DIFFERENT KINDS OF DEFORMERS?

There are a ton of deformation tools in Maya. I have created subcategories of types to make it easier to identify the numerous tools for deformation in multiple software packages. Since deformation is so essential to the primary function of modern character animation, the amount of variation on it is dizzying, but if you start to learn the simple constructs you will see that they all work on similar principles.

7.2.1 Node-Based Deformers

Node-based deformers are shapes that change the proportional appearance of your object based on some mathematical transformations in space. They "warp" your geometry in some manner that resembles a physical action, usually described by the title of the deformer. "Bend," "Twist," and "Flare" are types of node-based deformers in Maya (known as nonlinear deformers). In Figure 7.1, you can see a few types of deformers applied to a fence post and the large amount of variety that can be produced. Node deformers are quick, clean, and simple ways of adjusting the shape of your model and animating it easily. The up side of node-based deformers is that they're quick, easy to set up and control, and can drastically change the appearance of your model with little effort. The down side is that they are not very complex and only offer a limited amount of control of the object shape. But they are the go-to method of making simple deformations in modeling as well as animation when you don't need anything more complex.

7.2.2 Point-Based Deformers

Point-based deformers use points in space, similar to vertices, to offset the locations of vertices that are grouped underneath them. In Maya, these

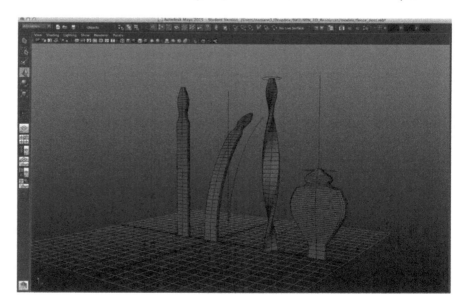

FIGURE 7.1   Different node-based deformers in action, changing the same fence-post geometry. The fence post has extra geometry, which ensures a smoother deformation.

FIGURE 7.2   A cluster is deforming these vertices with different cluster weights assigned to them, which makes them deform unevenly. The cluster is represented by a "c."

are called "Clusters," which are just null nodes that can change the movement of a vertex or group of vertices based on the transform of that cluster. The most important aspect of the cluster node is that it can have "weights" assigned to it for each vertex, which allows its influence upon the vertices assigned to it be spread out or adjusted on a per-vertex level. Figure 7.2 shows a polygon plane, assigned to a cluster in which the weights of that cluster have been painted unevenly across the center of the plane, illustrating how transforming the cluster will offset each vertex according to its cluster weight value. The clusters, having their own transform node, can then be parented, grouped, have their pivots edited, and controlled through expressions or other means, which will in turn change the shape node of the polygon they are influencing. This is a primitive method of "skinning," which we will look at in detail in the next chapter.

7.2.3 Lattice Deformers

Lattices are essentially "cages" or cubes without shading in-between the vertices. These lattices can be subdivided like a primitive cube as many times as preferred, each time giving a higher level of control over the object to be deformed. Each "Lattice Point" has a transform, just like a polygon vertex, and moving that point will proportionately deform the object based on the distance of the polygonal vertex (or NURBS CV) to that point. In this way a lattice can create very specific deformations of a targeted area in a very specific way. It can easily produce several "versions" of a character while retaining the same basic geometry. Specific groups of vertices can have a lattice applied, including vertices from multiple objects, which makes it easy to ensure consistent deformation even across several surfaces without destroying the continuity. Lattice points can be animated or driven by other values and used in a rigging situation, although they tend to be used for modeling more often.

Lattices work by using a "base" copy, which is a duplicate with the same number of lattice points that remains invisible underneath. The lattice point that you move then creates an offset from the original position (being kept in the base copy) and the offset is applied to the vertices or NURBS CVs proportional to the distance they are from the lattice point. The further away they are, the less they are affected by the lattice point that you are moving. This makes the deformation smoothly applied, which allows for multitudes of custom changes to a model without having to move each vertex independently. Lattices are vital for making smooth global tweaks to an area of a high-density model quickly! In Figure 7.3, you can see how a simple lattice was able to convert our normal character into a pudgier one.

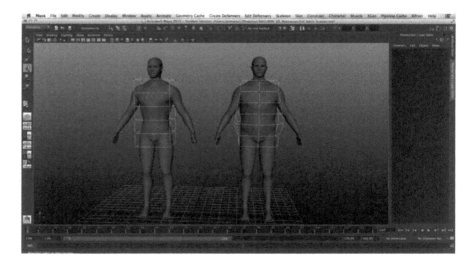

FIGURE 7.3 The figure on the left had a lattice applied to the vertices of the torso and those lattice points were adjusted, giving us the slightly pudgier character on the right but retaining the same exact geometry and number of vertices.

7.2.4 Curve-Based Deformers

Curve-based deformers use curves (NURBS in Maya) to generate deformations on vertices or NURBS CVs. A Wire deformer is much like a Lattice Deformer, but instead of polygonal-like points and a cage it uses a base curve and an offset curve. In Figure 7.4, you can see the results of applying a Wire Deformer to a polygon plane, where the offset of the wire curve deforms the vertices based on the distance from the curve itself. This is a really good tool to create bulges or surface offsets in only one small area, resembling a skin pulled over a wire.

7.2.5 Geometry-Based Deformers

Geometry-based deformers are deformers that use one piece of geometry to influence another one. There are several geometry-based deformers in Maya and each one of them has specific parameters and functions that are useful.

"Sculpt" deformers are when one object asserts influence upon another one as a "pusher" or a "puller," pulling the surface in the positive direction of the surface normal or pushing on it in the negative direction of the surface normal. Figure 7.5 illustrates how a poly sphere can influence the shape of a poly plane by displacing it based on the shape of the sphere—it creates an indent in the center, like putting a bowling ball in a taut sheet!

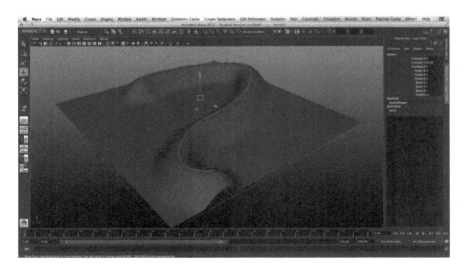

FIGURE 7.4 A Wire Deformer offsetting vertices from a polygon plane with a NURBS curve.

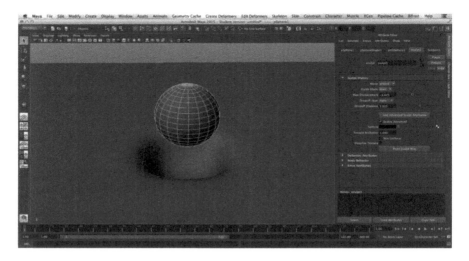

FIGURE 7.5   A sculpt deformer, using a sphere to deform a plane.

"Wrap" deformers also use geometry to deform geometry, but in this case an inner influence object influences an outer geometry object, as if one of them were "wrapped" around another one, attempting to maintain the shape of the inner object. This deformer is generally used to create a high-resolution layer of deformation on top of a lower-resolution object, such as a character model. This allows the deformation of the low-resolution character to drive the high-resolution character, making the rigging job easier and offering a way to add a layer of skin-like behavior to an otherwise clunky model, smoothing out the kinks. In Figure 7.6, you can see that a high-resolution, pill-like model has been deformed with a low-resolution model, which is where the vertex offsets are actually taking place. This allows a low-resolution model to control a high-resolution model smoothly.

"Blend Shapes," also known in other software packages as "Morph Targets," deserve special mention here as an important aspect of character deformation. Blend shapes use one or more "Targets," which are based on the "Base Shape," to create a vertex offset that moves the Base Shape vertices to the exact same positions of the Target vertices in a linear manner. This creates the illusion that the vertices are morphing from one position to another. The two targets *should* have the exact same vertices with the exact same vertex array indices, but it's possible to have two that don't (although I would highly advise making your blend shapes congruent).

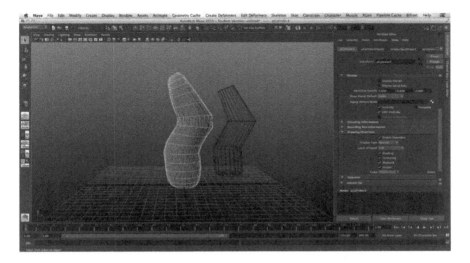

FIGURE 7.6 Low-resolution polygon model on the right controls the shape of the high-resolution model on the left based on the manipulation of its vertices (the shape on the right is extracted to the side so you can see it better).

If the previous statements make no sense whatsoever to you, then think of it this way—making a series of blend shapes is like pulling and pushing on a piece of clay you keep duplicating. Each expression can be morphed to from the base shape, giving the animator the ability to create face animations rapidly. Blend shapes are also really good for creating corrective areas for skinning, which we will visit later.

Blend Shapes are edited with a blend shape slider, which has a value of 0–1 for each Target Shape. A value of zero means that the Target Shape has zero influence on the vertices of the Base Shape. A value of 1 means that the Target Shape has 100% of influence over the Base Shape, blended with the total sum of all other Target Shapes affecting it (Figure 7.7).

"Jiggle" is a useful deformer that creates a physics-based "jiggle" or secondary motion for your character based on the primary motion of the skeleton. It's not actually physics based, but sets up a delay action for "jiggly" parts of your character like female breasts, antennae, or fat rolls on a portly character. It is set up much like a cluster, with weights and parameters that control the action of the jiggle.

"Skinning" is the final deformer type we need to understand and it's such a big part of character rigging that I have devoted the entire next chapter to understanding, creating, and editing a skin. A skin is what takes the skeletal transforms and applies them to the vertices in a proportional

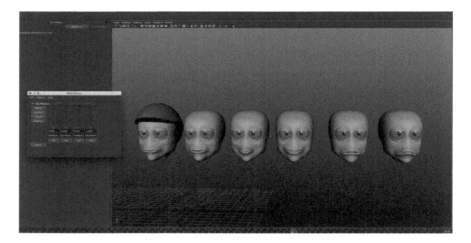

FIGURE 7.7 **(See color insert.)** Blend shape targets for a cartoon head lined up in a row. The shape on the far left is the Base Shape and all the rest are targets that the base shape will "morph" to when the slider values are adjusted (character head model by artist Fred Mathis).

manner—much like the Cluster deformer. It allows the vertices to be deformed based on skeletal movements with each vertex receiving a weight value from each joint in the skin, allowing you to have more than one joint influencing each vertex. Editing the skin weights in Maya is done with a painting tool called "Artisan," which is used in multiple capacities in other places in Maya. Please read Chapter 8 to understand all the aspects of skin weights that you need to know in order to set your model up properly for fully articulated character animation.

7.3 HOW ARE DEFORMERS USED IN MODELING, ANIMATING, AND CHARACTER RIGGING?

As you have seen, there are many, many types of deformers to use in 3D animation, and they have many different applications as modeling and animation tools. They are invaluable for tweaking the shape of a model, offering the flexibility to deform the entire piece of geometry as a whole, or just edit a single, isolated area. They can also be used to create simple animation action without the use of bones—a bending reed, a ripple on the surface of water, or an animal crawling beneath a sheet could all be created using simple animated deformers, and thus avoid joints and skeletons altogether.

In character rigging, there are three passes of deformation: the primary skin, the secondary "corrective" deformations, and the tertiary physics-based action (like jiggle). The primary deformation is based on the major skeletal joint movement and is created using the skin. The secondary corrective deformation is to smooth out the primary deformation, create muscle-like "stretchy" appearances, deform muscular action like biceps flexing, and generally provide a higher level of realism. Tertiary action is usually used to simulate physics and soft actions like cloth, hair, and fat jiggles. There can be all sorts of levels in-between, but these three are usually present in some capacity, if not at *least* the primary and secondary.

CHAPTER 8

Skinning a Character

8.1 WHAT IS SKINNING?

"Skinning" a character is a term you will hear a lot when it comes to character rigging. It means that you are going to create a deformation method for the joints in a skeleton to control the movement of the vertices in a character mesh or meshes. Skinning allows the transforms of the joints to control the vertex offset, based on the pivot point of the joint. It is the primary method of deformation for any character using joints.

8.2 HOW DOES SKINNING WORK?

Skinning is a special kind of a deformer that works exclusively with Joints and polygon vertices or NURBS CVs. It creates a "skin cluster," which is a fancy form of a Cluster Deformer, but instead of using Cluster handles, it simply uses the joints as the clusters. When you "bind" the model to the skeleton, a database spreadsheet is created of every vertex in the model and every joint in the skeleton. "Skin weights" are values that are created for each vertex, for each joint in the skin cluster. Each vertex in the model will have a list of joints that is influencing it. Although you can have every single joint in a skeleton influencing every single vertex (even if its influence is zero), it is also possible to have only the pertinent joints influencing the vertices it needs to, and not the ones it doesn't. For technical reasons and a matter of personal preference I prefer that *all* joints in a skeleton have an influence over *all* vertices in the pertinent model, even if that influence is zero. Contrary to my usual way of working, this is actually *less* efficient in terms of overall data, but in my opinion, simpler to work with, to edit, and to transfer weights from one model to another.

When a model is "bound" to a skeleton using some type of skinning method, a skin cluster is created and added to the geometry in the History. A "Bind Pose" is also created, which saves the values of the Joint transforms in order to pop back into this original pose if need be by using the "Go to Bind Pose" option. Note that in Maya, the bind pose cannot be returned to if IK or some other node is controlling the transforms of the joints in any way (you can disable the IK in order to get back to the bind pose).

The spreadsheet of data that Maya uses to keep all the skin weights in order is available in the "Component Editor," as you can see in Figure 8.1. Each vertex is listed in the rows and each Joint influence is listed in the columns. That's a lot of columns and rows! Trying to edit weights with the Component Editor is a little tedious—but we have much better tools to do this. I just wanted you to be familiar with the mechanism under the hood. Every vertex has an influence from every joint—but all of those influences added together *must* equal a total of 1.0. This is called "normalization." Whenever you decrease the influence of one joint, the other joints must increase influence to even out the loss. Conversely, when you increase the influence of one joint over a vertex, the others will be reduced. Now, since not *all* the joints in the influence have a weight value over zero, only the ones with a weight value of over zero will be reduced. This is not true for

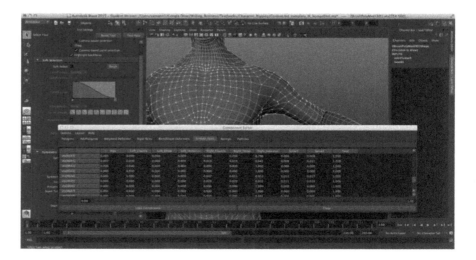

FIGURE 8.1 **(See color insert.)** The Component Editor showing all of the details about the selected vertices and the skin weight values listed for each joint.

reducing weights on a vertex for a given joint; however—in this case we don't have an absolutely clear indication of which joints might receive the added value. It could be *any* joint in the list. There are methods to reduce the possibilities, and make sure that it only happens to the joints that you choose; however, it is still somewhat of an unknown factor. For this reason, the best way to edit your skin weights is to strictly use increases in weights from one joint to another—and never decrease it (decreasing will happen naturally on joints already set up with influence). This is not an easy thing to grasp at first—but if you stick to the fundamental progression that I lay out, you will have the most success.

8.3 WHAT ARE THE DIFFERENT TYPES OF SKINNING METHODS?

Every software package has their own idiosyncrasies; however, in Maya there are three main types of bindings (which are all variations on the same basic thing): "rigid" binding, "smooth" binding, and "interactive" binding.

Rigid binding is somewhat of an anachronism, and indeed the older true rigid bind isn't even an option in the newer versions of Maya, but it deserves some mention because handheld game systems, web-based games, and mobile games often make use of this low-overhead system where only a single joint can have influence over a vertex at a time. Calculating every joint value for every vertex takes some kind of memory and processing overhead, and limiting the possibilities to only one joint influence per vertex can save a ton of resources. The down side is that there is no "soft" or "smooth" bind, and polygons can have rough edges or ragged results in bend areas like elbows and knees. The up side is that it's really easy to work with and extremely fast to calculate, which makes a difference if you want those frame rates at 60 Hz or higher! Although Maya got rid of the true rigid bind system a while back, you can mimic the effect by making a smooth bind and flooding weights with zero values for everything except one joint influence per vertex (in fact we'll do just that for several areas).

Smooth binding is the most common and flexible form of skin binding in Maya—it uses multiple weights per vertex, which are adjustable using a toolset called "Artisan," which allows you to "paint" skin weight values in an organic fashion, saving you the trouble of having to tweak those values inside a big spreadsheet. Artisan can help the artist visualize the influence value of the joints to the vertex using a grayscale color method—the vertices will light up white with a value of 1 and black with a value of 0, allowing the artist to "paint" these values with a virtual brush. We will be exploring

Artisan a little later and in greater detail in the lesson at the end of this chapter. Smooth binding seeks to "autoskin" or set smooth skin weights to your model based on proximity to the joints of the vertices, among multiple other methods. Most of these are poorly executed, and any decent character rigger is going to have their individual methodology for generating and editing skin weights. The important thing to remember is that Maya or any other software can't really do a good job at autoskinning—you have to do this by hand! Otherwise you get a "mushy" character, or one that has too many small weights on vertices that don't need the influences. The only way to edit these skin weights is to use Artisan or the Component Editor (Figure 8.2).

Interactive binding is somewhat new to Maya and actually somewhat based on a method from Autodesk's other major software, 3D Studio Max. Skin weights are assigned using "Envelopes" or capsules that emanate from each joint, allowing the artist to tweak the values by visualizing volume instead of color values. It's not nearly precise as traditional skin weight editing, however, it's way easier to get a ballpark bind with some detail. The nice thing about interactive binding is that it's technically still a smooth bind—you can then further tweak the skin weights with the Artisan tool, also known as the Pain Skin Weights Tool. Interactive Binding uses a kind of "heat map" or color-based interaction to show you how much influence the capsule has over the affected vertices, as you can see in Figure 8.3.

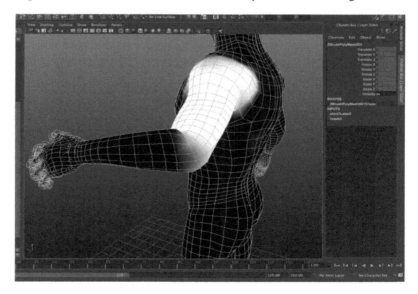

FIGURE 8.2 **(See color insert.)** The light and dark areas of an Artisan toolset allowing the artist to paint joint influences organically.

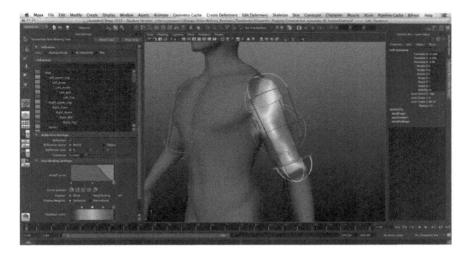

FIGURE 8.3 **(See color insert.)** The Interactive Binding method, which has capsules that use volume influence to control how much influence a joint has over the vertices inside it.

8.4 WHAT ARE THE IMPORTANT PARAMETERS OF BINDING A CHARACTER?

When binding a character, there are several keys parameters that can drastically change the way that you visualize, edit, and adjust the skin weights. These key parameters must usually be set *before* you make the bind, because many of them cannot be changed (or at least *shouldn't* be changed) after the initial bind of weights.

Binding to a joint hierarchy or selected joints gives you the option to choose specific joints to bind your model to, or use every joint in the hierarchy. While I generally use every joint in the hierarchy for a full body model, I often use just a selected joint for places where you only need one joint as an influence—for instance, a hat on a character's head. It only needs to be bound to the head joint, so why bother putting any other joints in the skin cluster?

The "Bind Method" is asking you which method you would like Maya to use in determining how exactly it will generate skin weights for the vertices automatically. Currently, the options are Closest Distance, Closest Hierarchy, Heat Map, and Geodesic Voxel. Each of these methods uses a different algorithm or mathematical formula to assign the skin weight values to your vertices. "Closest distance" uses the closest distance of the joint pivot point to the vertex to determine the weight value, a method which can often times result in inappropriate weights for certain joints since they will be closer than others to the vertex, but unlikely to influence that part of the body. For instance, the left leg would not influence vertices in the right thigh but the proximity of those vertices to the leg makes it likely to happen using this bind method. "Closest in Hierarchy" seeks to prevent this from happening by using the joint hierarchy (and to some degree distance) to determine the skin weights. This method is far more stable and is the default setting. "Heat maps" use an algorithmic falloff diffusion, where the closer to the joint the vertex is, the "hotter" the value, and the further away the "cooler." This is very similar to the Interactive Bind, but you can't edit the capsules to adjust it. "Geodesic Voxel" binding uses the volume of a particular polygon object to create "voxels," which are volumetric objects that will fill up the space of the geometry and inherit the weights from the skeleton, and then transfer them onto the character model itself. This is for lower-polygon models in which the geometry is not divided into enough vertices to get smooth transitions with the other three methods.

Just a note here that no matter *what* option you choose to let Maya autoweight your model, you will have to manually set your skin weights anyway, getting rid of anything generated here. Although Maya will generate skin weights for you, it's not really suggested or recommended to leave them that way. In fact, my lesson for this chapter will instruct you to remove the autoweighting altogether and create your own from scratch.

"Skinning method" is the set of calculations with which the transforms of the vertices will be determined when you rotate a joint. "Classic Linear" will use an older, linear method of transforming the vertices with the joint by multiplying the skin weight times the transform of each joint it's being influenced by and offsetting the vertex value blended between its influencing joints accordingly. It's the most commonly used method. "Dual Quaternion" is another method, which is designed to preserve the volume of your character, even in a "twisting" joint like the wrist or the Humerus. It had its own characteristics that makes it behave quite differently than classic linear; however, it's fabulous for low-resolution character rigs that lack twists nodes and need the best deformation possible for the lowest cost. Dual quaternion skinning is sometimes used in LOD characters and low-node skeleton characters. Weight blended offers the best of both worlds—you can blend your skin weights between Classic Linear (for non-twisting areas) and Dual Quaternion (for twisting and areas where volume loss is common) by painting areas to use one or the other or a blend of both. This is a fairly new feature, albeit a fabulous one since both types of skinning methods offer useful properties in specific areas of a character.

"Normalizing" weights is the setting that tells Maya to automatically normalize or ensure that your weights always equal zero. As we discussed previously, you can add or remove weight influence from one joint, and the normalization will adjust all of the other weights in order to equal the total to a value of 1. The default value is to be set to on, however you can entirely disable it, allowing for values of over 1 (which allow you to exaggerate specific areas or overcompensate). "Post" will normalize the weights only when you specify, which means that you can preserve the previous skin weights before running a full normalize.

"Weight Distribution" is the option that tells Maya how you want it to proceed in the act of normalization. When you decrease the skin weight value on a joint, it must compensate by increasing the weights on other joints. The two options here are Distance and Neighbors. Distance will add influence to a vertex purely based on distance from the influencing joints, while neighbors will use the hierarchy. This option, when using my specific skin weight methodology, is completely unnecessary since I recommend never *reducing* the influence weight from a joint, but only *adding* to one. In the lesson for this chapter, you will see how this works.

Allowing multiple bind poses means that a single skeleton can be bound to multiple meshes and contains multiple bind poses—if this is not checked, the smooth bind action will not bind a model to a skeleton if that skeleton is not in the bind pose generated for the initial model bound to it.

"Maximum Influences" is the maximum number of joints in a skin cluster that can affect any given vertex at a time. Maintain maximum influences will maintain this number when normalization is taking place as you are editing the skin weights.

"Removed Unused Influences" will remove any joints from the influence list of a vertex—for instance, there's no reason that a head joint should be in the list for a vertex in the toe of the character! While it is much more efficient to have this setting checked, I generally leave it off for the same reasons that I bind every vertex to every joint in a model, even if it won't have influence on it—it makes the copy, transfer, and export of skin weights easier to accomplish.

"Colorize skeleton" will colorize the wireframe draws of your joints to match the colors in the Paint Skin Weights Tool. I personally find it distracting, but it doesn't really matter which you prefer.

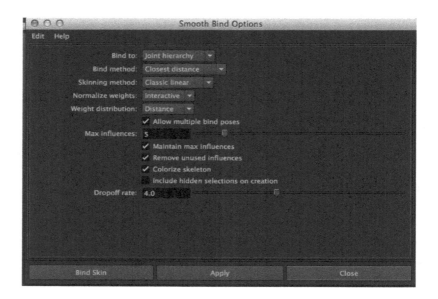

FIGURE 8.4   Options Box for Smooth Binding a mesh to a skeleton.

"Include hidden selections on creating" is an option that will bind any selected but invisible geometry to the skeleton. Generally this should be set to "On," and it is a good thing to note that the behavior of Maya has changed in the most recent versions (2014 and up) to *not* bind objects that are not visible unless this box is checked.

"Dropoff Rate," or "Heatmap Falloff" are the settings for the falloff ratio of weighting with either the closest distance/closes in hierarchy or the Heat Map methods, respectively. Once again, this isn't that important if you intend to manually edit the skin weights yourself (and we are) (Figure 8.4).

8.5 CAN I LET MAYA DO MY SKIN WEIGHTS FOR ME?

No! Let me just say that again—*absolutely not*! And one more time, just to be sure you understand—*you can't expect the initial weights to be perfect, good, or even acceptable by any decent standard.* I have spent up to 4 months tweaking skin weights on a single character. There is no true "autoskin," and any decent rigger will spend a good portion of his or her time on editing the skin weights by hand. My system, as you will see in detail in the lesson for this chapter, relies on custom skin-weight editing that does not use Maya's autoweights at all.

8.6 WHAT IS ARTISAN?

Artisan is the tool that Maya uses to paint things in 3D space with a virtual brush, much like Photoshop allows you to do on a 2D canvas. Maya can create a brush that will adhere to the surface of your character and paint values on it for different things, including skin weights. It is the primary tool for editing, tweaking, and polishing skin weights on a bound character. The Paint Skin Weights Tool is an offshoot of Artisan. It's the tool that most character riggers use to tweak values of the weight influence from the joint to the vertex. This tool uses a visible grayscale value to indicate the amount of influence a particular joint has over a vertex. These per-vertex values display in the 3D view for each joint selected in the list. You can then "paint" the weights with a virtual brush, with one of the four operations: "add," "subtract," "replace," and "smooth." Add weights will add the value, multiplied by the opacity (from 0 to 1 on both values) to the vertex's weight influence for the joint selected in the list. This, due to normalization, will cause the other influences of joints on the vertex to reduce by enough value to ensure that the total influence remains at 1 (provided normalization is on and interactive). "Add" is the safest operator and indeed the only one I ever use, since it will never add weight to any unspecified joint (for instance, adding head joint influence values to the foot). Because of normalization, painting with an operator of Add and a value of 1.0 is the exact same thing as Replacing with a value of 1.0. If all weights must add up to 1, then adding with a value of 1 will set all the rest to zero!

"Scale" is an operator that subtracts value from the selected joint and the painted vertex. In that subtraction, however, more value to joint influence weights or indeed more joint influences could occur, because it's not always clear to Maya *which* joint to add the weights when you subtract them from another joint. To be sure, Maya is pretty smart about it and rarely throws joint influence weights onto improper joints, but in nontraditional rigs this could be a problem; I avoid it for this reason altogether.

"Smooth" will blend the weight values from surrounding vertices onto the painted vertex, in effect "smoothing" out the change in values between two vertices. I also eschew this function, useful though it may seem, in order to avoid similar problems to the Scale Operator—it often puts weights where I don't want them.

"Replace" will replace the weight of the painted vertex for the selected joint, engaging normalization to set all the other weights to the appropriate values or even adding to new joint influences if the replaced value is less than the initial value. Once again, I avoid this entirely. Trying to eradicate weights on a vertex for a particular joint by replacing them with zero is like rolling a set of dice and saying you want it to end up with a total value of 10—you may get it but there are a dozen combinations to reach that result. In other words, I avoid it entirely.

The key to proper skin weighting, as you will see in Chapter 8 Lesson, is to only blend the weights by painting in the areas that need them! You can avoid a lot of work and trouble by reminding yourself that only certain areas have blended values. Much of the body will be hard-weighted, or to a value of 1.0 for a specific joint. Of the areas that aren't set to a single joint influence, most of them are going to be using only two joints as influences. Only a very few will have three joints influencing them, and almost *none* have four. There are exceptions to this in advanced, "muscle-based" rigs, but even in those having more than three, influences per joint can get very dodgy (Figure 8.5).

FIGURE 8.5 **(See color insert.)** The Artisan Interface for skinning weights on a smooth bound character.

8.7 WHAT IF I NEED TO MOVE A JOINT AFTER SKINNING MY CHARACTER?

Moving a joint, postweighting, is a delicate enterprise. Any transforms that occur to a joint will subsequently affect the vertices and offset from the Bind Pose. So what are our options?

One answer to this dilemma is the Move Skinned Joints Tool. It allows you to quickly move a joint (in world space coordinates) to a different position and see how that change will affect the deformation. Often times the joint needs to be tweaked and tested in different positions, since that can drastically change the nature of your deformation by changing the pivot point from which the vertices receive their offsets. Since every model is slightly different, there's no good way to do this universally, and tweaking and testing is the best way to ensure the best result. Note that when Maya lets you move or adjust the joint, its children do not inherit this change—it moves *only* the joint you have selected. Another thing to note about the Move Skinned Joints Tool is that moving the joint in any direction *but* the primary axis will result in an incorrect joint orient! If you move the joint on any other axis than the primary, the primary axis will no longer aim toward the child. So the best option is to either move it only along that primary axis (we are using the Y-axis, in case you forgot) or do it the manual way (after this you can reorient the joints). Another limitation of this tool is that you can't mirror the joint position changes automatically. You must do the other side manually (Figure 8.6).

8.8 HOW CAN I SAVE MY SKIN WEIGHTS SO I HAVE TO DO THEM AGAIN?

We can adjust bound joints by unbinding the mesh, move the joints, and then re-bind the skin and paint the skin weights again. But that's just a waste of time. Who wants to do the same thing twice? Re-painting weights is a long process. What we really need is a way to export the skin weights so that we can repeat the process, but without the tedium. Maya has an Export Skin Weight Maps, which allow us to export the current vertex skin weights to a series of texture maps, based on the object UV's. The biggest caveat to this method is the fact that it writes out a single texture map for *each* joint, making it a large data set. Another major flaw in this manner of saving skin weights is the fact that the texture maps are based on object UV coordinates. If you don't have any UV mapping on the character, this method of saving skin weights is completely useless.

A better way of going about saving weights, and indeed one I prefer to use, is to save a per-vertex weight list, based on the weight cluster. Unfortunately this

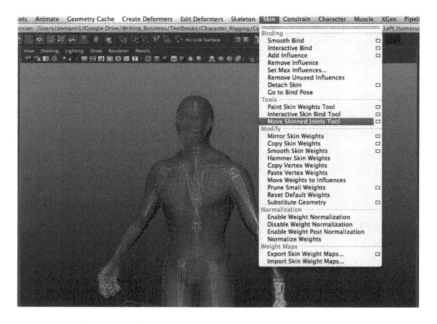

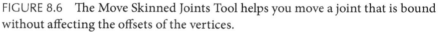

FIGURE 8.6   The Move Skinned Joints Tool helps you move a joint that is bound without affecting the offsets of the vertices.

has never been natively supported by Maya, but there are several third-party plugins out there which perform this very function. It's also not too incredibly hard to write a script yourself if you're familiar with Python or MEL.

Another option, if you don't want to bother with exporting or importing your skin weights, is using the "Copy Skin Weights Tool." Maya allows you to copy skin weights from one model to another, provided they are bound to the same skeleton and relatively close together in physical volume/space. In order to tweak the joint positions you can edit them with the Envelope set to 0, which will turn off the deformation, then duplicate the old model, bind it to the skeleton (deleting the initial bind pose first), then copy the skin weights from the old model to the new model, finally deleting the old model. This is not the most efficient way of going about things (indeed it leaves some artifacts in the Hypergraph) but it will work for this purpose very well. You will get an adjusted skeleton binding the same model with the same skin weights.

8.9 WHAT IS SECONDARY AND TERTIARY DEFORMATION?

If skin weights are the Primary method of deformation, Secondary deformation is "corrective" or enhancing what the skin weighting is already doing for you. Since we can only get so much detail from a pure skin weighting, we often must correct difficult areas or add in muscle-based joints to create a more realistic appearance to our character. There are many, many techniques to do this, but the primary focus in the following chapters will be using corrective blend shapes, which correct the skin weighting on a vertex-to-vertex basis, allowing you to really sculpt and fine-tune the areas that need it as well as make the musculature of the character pop out and respond to the skeletal movements.

Tertiary deformers are generally based on physics, where the jiggle and soft bounciness are important, like cloth, breasts, fat rolls, antennae, and anything else that has some level of pliability and responds to physical force. Because they are unique to each character, I am only mentioning them in passing to make you aware of them, but we won't be covering their use in this book since it would qualify as an intermediate or even advanced use of deformers. Deformation is layered, so as you learn you can add these on top of the skin weights and the corrective blends.

So now we have been through the major concepts of skin weights, skin weight editing tools, and weighting options. This is the second pillar of a character rigger's job! Arguably, it's the last vestige of the area that hasn't been entirely overrun with automatic solutions (like the Edit Rigs and skeletons) because there is so much variation on the model that it's hard to have a universal solution (although I'm sure it'll happen eventually). For a better understanding of how to tackle this particular task step-by-step in more detail, make sure to follow through the lesson at the end of this chapter.

8.10 LESSON 1: THE ZEMAN SKIN WEIGHT METHOD

OK, so here we are, embarking on the Zeman Skin Weights Methodology. After 15 years of painting skin weights I have come up with a workflow that's efficient and requires the *least* amount of time and effort with the *most* reliable results. It requires that you follow the steps laid out in the correct sequence, and do things exactly as suggested. If you do this you will find that you can quickly and reliably create good basic skin weights on a character, which can then be tweaked and edited with more advanced rigging solutions, like muscle joints, corrective blend shapes, etc.

The most important thing to take away from this methodology is that if the basic weighting is correct, and there aren't minuscule weights floating all over the place, then your job is going to be far easier as the rig and skinning solution gets more and more complex. We don't want complexity in the weighting model—the less options you have for joint influences on a skin the easier your job will be. Once again, the skin weighting is the heart of what makes a successful character rig!

8.10.1 Step 1: Binding the Character to the Skeleton

I am using my human character model and my basic skeleton with a single twist node in the forearm. Check out the last lesson in this book for a more detailed twist rig. We want to make sure that the skeleton and the model are in the proper position, and make sure that we freeze and reset the transforms on the character model (see Figure 8.7). Freezing and resetting the transforms of a character model will reset the vertex xyz values in Model Space to zero, which will make sure that our skin cluster transforms are starting out from an unaltered state.

Also make sure that *all* joints have rotation values of zero. If we have IK handles setup (and generally I like to do my IK *after* the skinning, but it's not necessary), then you need to disable the IK and make sure you set all of your joints to Euler XYZ values of zero. You want the "Bind Pose" to be this exact pose—with the rotation values of zero for all joints. This way you can easily go back to the bind pose later, when the IK and rigging

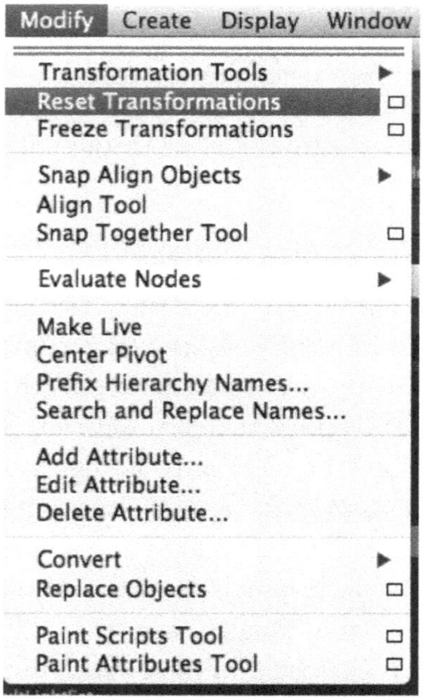

FIGURE 8.7 Freeze and Reset transforms on all geometry you intend to bind (but not the skeleton!).

inputs keep Maya from automatically assuming the bind pose through the "go to bind pose" command.

Select the root of the skeleton and the model or models and go to Skin → Smooth Bind. Use the exact parameters as shown in Figure 8.8 to bind the model. Some of these options are very important, and others not so important. Make sure that normalize is set to interactive and that you are binding to the entire skeleton, not just selected joints.

Now, provided that everything has processed properly, you will get a smooth bind! There are a few reasons that this might not happen or throw an error; the most common of which are listed in the following:

1. If you don't have a model *and* a joint is selected, Maya won't know what to bind.

2. If any of the geometry you have selected is already bound to a skin cluster, Maya will throw an error saying it is already bound to a skeleton.

3. If the skeleton has a bind pose and it is not *in* that bind pose when you try to bind it, it will throw an error. This is common when having more than one model bound to the same skeleton and when you are moving joints after the bind to tweak deformation properties.

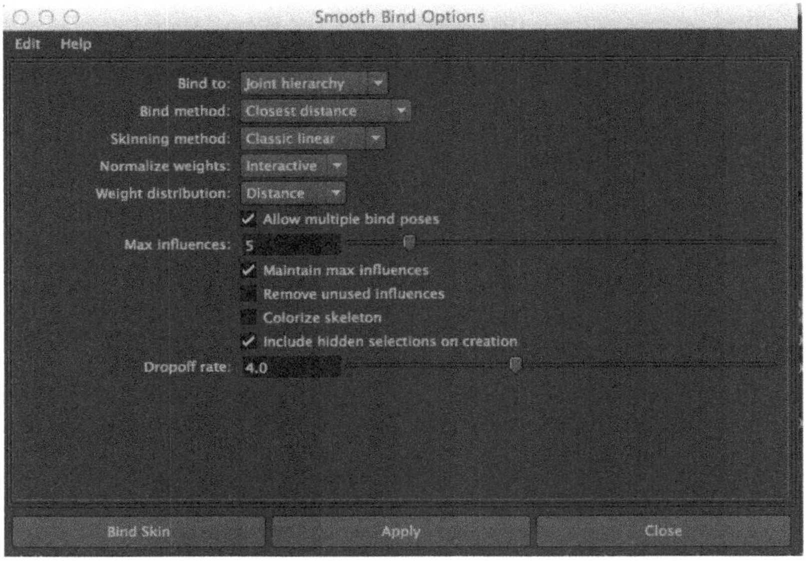

FIGURE 8.8   The correct settings for our initial smooth bind.

Now we have a bind on our model! You can test this out by rotating your joints, one at a time, just to check it out. No matter what method of skin weight application we have used, there will be all kinds of discrepancies and errors in the original skin weighting—this isn't a problem, because in the next section we're going to fix it manually.

8.10.2 Step 2: Blocking Out Skin Weights

This step is like wielding a giant paintbrush with white paint. What we want to do is flood all of the vertices in a certain area with a value of 1.0 influence for a single joint. Instead of trying to smooth or blend weights, we really want to whitewash them to a single joint to begin with, delineating the separations with hard edges to begin our weighting process. This eliminates all of the fractional weights in the vertex influence values, and it sets hard areas that are only influenced by a single joint. Although human skin is pliable and flexible, most of that flexibility and stretchiness is focused on the seams between one joint and another—the majority of the deformative action of the skin is assigned to a single joint only. If you have too many weights from too many joints affecting your vertices, the skin will be "mushy" and not very characteristic of a real human body.

Blocking out weights is a fairly simple process. You select the vertices of the character you want to block, go to the Paint Skin Weights Tool, and flood replace them with a value of 1.0 for the intended joint. The first step is to do this to the entire model at once with the root node being the selected joints influence. Keep in mind that this will completely remove *all* weight influences from *all* other joints! This is what we want, as shown in Figure 8.9.

Now that the entire model is complete, we can begin on the rest. The key here is to select the area of vertices that will be associated with each "section" of the body that corresponds to a certain joint. We do this in a hierarchical manner, from highest to lowest, just to make it easy to do the selections. So the next section we'll do is the first spine joint.

Select the vertices that correspond to this joint spatially, in this case the center of the character. Since we'll be mirroring the skin weights, it's not necessary to select both sides evenly! In fact, it's actually way easier to make the vertex selection on one side only, as in Figure 8.10.

Now we will "flood" those vertices with a value of 1.0 for the Spine 1 joint, as you can see in Figure 8.11. This will get us a solid area of influence for the center spine joint.

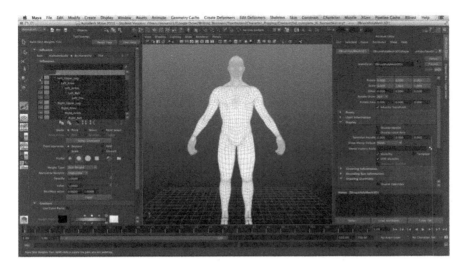

FIGURE 8.9   The weights flooded to a value of 1.0 to the root joint on the character model.

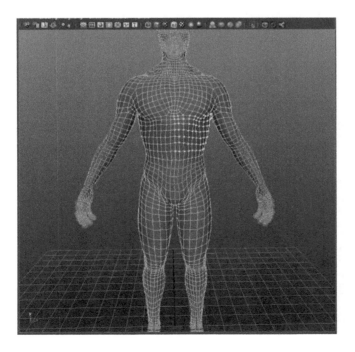

FIGURE 8.10   Selecting vertices on one side of the middle spine area to flood.

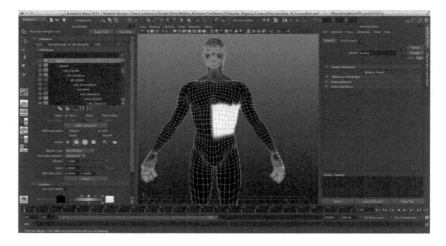

FIGURE 8.11 The flooded weights on one side.

Now we can select the entire piece of geometry and mirror the skin weights using the options in Figure 8.12. Mirroring the skin weights will do exactly that—ensure that the skin weights are even on the opposite side. We use the YZ plane, provided that the character is facing the positive Z-axis. The surface association should be perfectly aligned if the character is symmetrical on both sides *and* the joints are perfectly mirrored on either side (Figure 8.13).

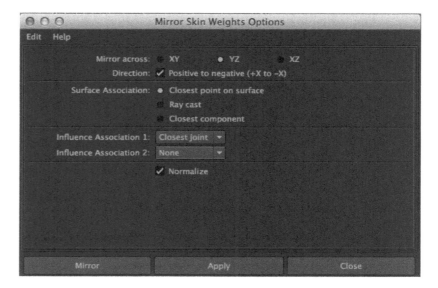

FIGURE 8.12 Mirror skin weights options.

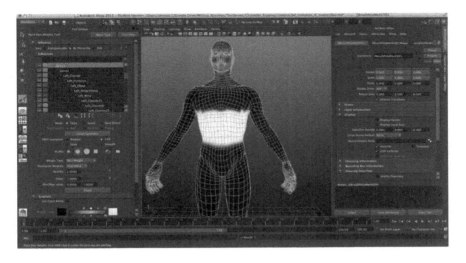

FIGURE 8.13 The mirrored result.

We use this process to go "down" the chain from the Spine 1 to the Head joints, selecting and flooding the vertices that are associated to that joint. It's OK to be a little messy since we will blend in areas later, but the important thing is that you follow the edge looping of the character and make sure that the skin weights are delineated from joint to joint in a straight line (see Figures 8.14 through 8.16).

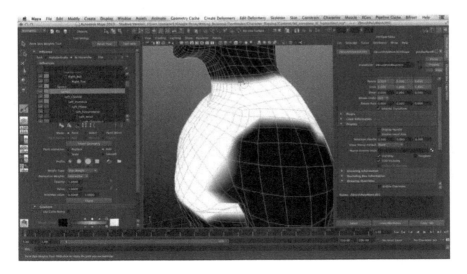

FIGURE 8.14 When blocking out skin weights, the best policy is to make your areas break at specific edge loops.

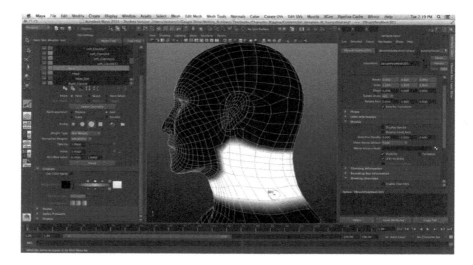

FIGURE 8.15   The break at the neck joint.

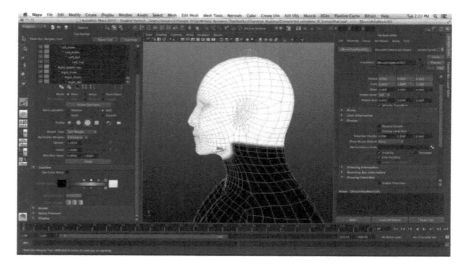

FIGURE 8.16   The break at the head joint.

Now the limbs get done in the same way—you select the entire limb vertices and flood them with a value of 1.0 (using Add) from the highest to the lowest in the hierarchy. This allows you to flood the entire selection of vertices as you go down the limb (Figures 8.17 through 8.20).

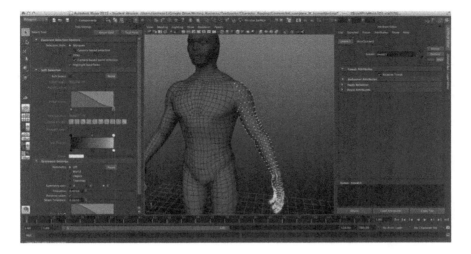

FIGURE 8.17　Selecting the vertices of the arm.

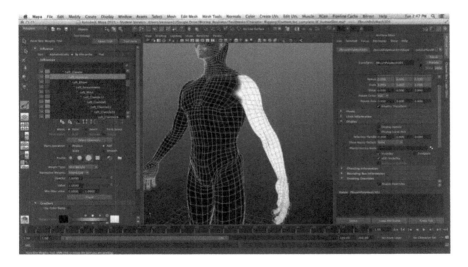

FIGURE 8.18　Flooding the vertices of the entire arm to the Humerus joint.

Of course, once you do the left arm you can proceed to the leg and then mirror the weights to the right side with the Mirror Skin Weights Action. A few things to note here—you don't need to do the Clavicle *just* yet, it's a special area that requires some work with blending weights from three influences (covered in the next step here).

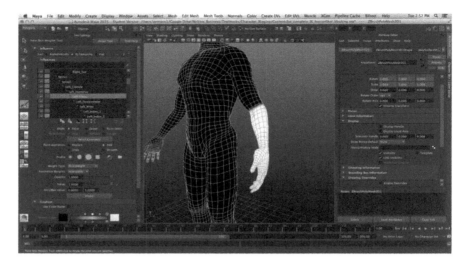

FIGURE 8.19 Selecting the vertices of the elbow and below and flooding them to the elbow.

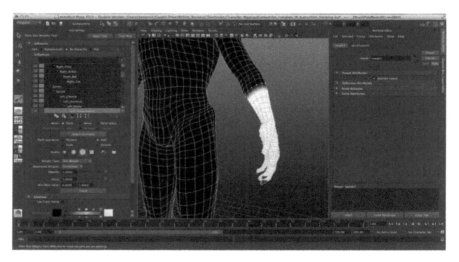

FIGURE 8.20 Repeating this process to the forearm twist. Note here that you would continue down the wrist, and then repeat this process for each finger.

8.10.3 Step 3: Blending the Weights in the Seams

Now that the entire model has been blocked out with the skin weights, we can concentrate on the areas where the skin weights really need to be painted—in the seams! The seams of the character are places like the elbow, wrist, forearm, and Humerus and Clavicle, Spine 3 areas where we have spread out the influences to smooth the vertices deformation influence. Let's start with the wrist and move our way up the arm.

The trick to blending the skin weights in the seam areas is to use the Add operator in the paint skin weights tool with a value of 0.1 or lower in the seams to tweak the values to blend properly.

First, rotate the joint we are working on slightly in one of its major ranges of motion. In Figure 8.21, you can see that I have rotated the wrist slightly in the X-axis.

Next, make sure that the Add operator is active, the Wrist joint influence is selected on the left-hand side, and that the Value of the operator is set to 0.1. If you begin to paint over the vertices with the left-mouse button down, you will see this value added to the skin weight influence value for the wrist joint. By swapping back and forth between the influence of a joint and its parent, you can change or adjust the blending of the skin weights in the seam easily. As you add small weight value to the rotated joint (in this case the wrist), the vertex will start to inherit the transform and the weight value will be reduced from the parent joint. When you paint influence for the parent (in this case the forearm twist), the vertex will move back to its original position in model space, reducing the influence weight from the rotated joint (the wrist). In the end you will find that only a few edge loops in the seam areas of the wrist and elbow need to be blended! Not only is this less

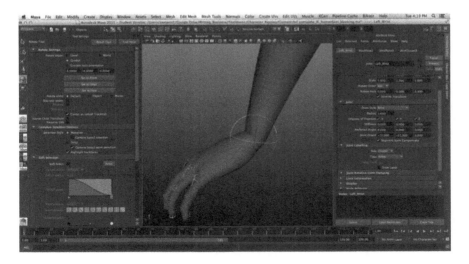

FIGURE 8.21. The wrist, rotated slightly on the X-axis in order to see the results of the skin weights as they are altered.

work for *you*, but it's also far more efficient in terms of data (for those real-time applications like mobile games).

Getting skin weights correctly painted is a skill that takes some experience and time—I can't tell you how many times I've gotten frustrated and started over on a character. I've come up with a few guidelines to make it easier to learn the first time around.

8.10.3.1 Don't Lose Volume

It's most important to preserve volume over avoiding interpenetration— the concept of skin "cleavage" is always a tough one, but it's important that the volume of a character area be preserved. The interpenetration of geometry can often times be scary, but trying to smooth out that area could force a loss of volume that is far less desirable than a "cleavage" area, which is actually a natural result of the folding of skin into skin. Figure 8.22 shows this in real life and Figure 8.23 is an example of this on the digital character. Figure 8.24 is an example of trying to tweak the weights in the vertices to avoid cleavage, but results in a loss of volume, which looks unnatural.

FIGURE 8.22   A real-life cleavage area where the skin presses together.

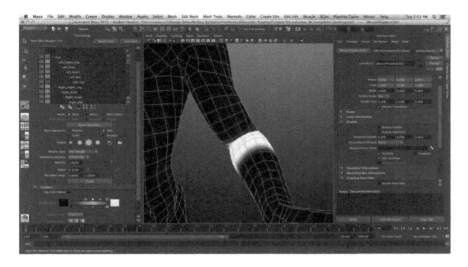

FIGURE 8.23 A digital example of the cleavage, where geometry interpenetrates geometry and creates a similar effect to skin.

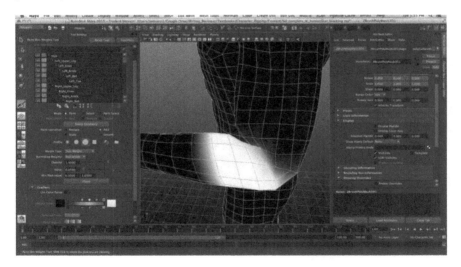

FIGURE 8.24 An incorrect way to deal with cleavage. By tweaking the skin weights too far onto one joint to avoid interpenetration, the forearm looks incorrect due to the loss of volume.

8.10.3.2 Weight for the Primary Axis of Motion First

When weighting your character, you should always rotate the joint on the primary axis of motion first and the weight for that movement. For instance, the wrist is mostly bent on the demo character in the X-axis in a range of ~90° in either direction; so this is what I will focus my initial weighting in. The wrist does move on the Z-axis of the character, but in a much tighter range of motion; so that is the secondary axis I focus on.

8.10.3.3 Avoid Unrealistic Ranges of Motion

Avoid putting limbs into extensively unrealistic positions and try to get the skin weights correct on them. In Figure 8.25, you can see the character leg, extended way too far beyond the natural range of motion. Often times there will be a trade-off to get the basic skin weights right for a range of motion—one direction will look fine, but the opposite will not. Pick the most important range of motion and make the weights work best for that one. It's most useful to make sure that the limbs are only rotated into realistic positions for skin weight adjusting in the seam areas (Figure 8.26).

8.10.3.4 Don't Get Too Caught up in Detailed Areas

It's easy to zoom into the microlevel and try to get every little curve to work with multiple positions of the joints. This can drive you crazy after a while and make you lose sight of the big picture. The character is usually going to be viewed on the screen from much further away than this—things that you agonize over on the microscopic level might never be an issue from

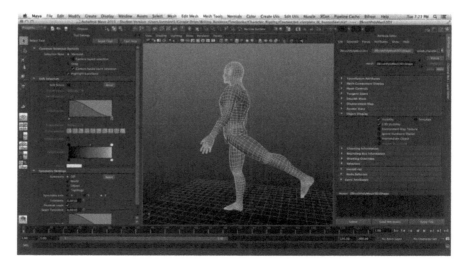

FIGURE 8.25   There's no way this character is ever going to be in this position, so trying to get the weights to look good in this direction is a waste of time!

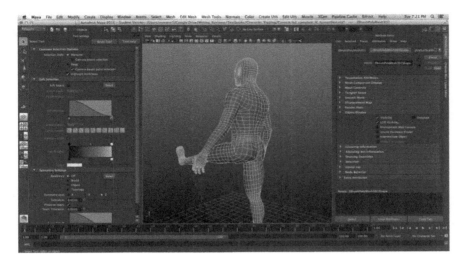

FIGURE 8.26 This position is far more likely to happen, so concentrate the weight values to look best here.

the final perspective; so take a minute to zoom out and relax a little bit. When the final character is textured, lit, and rendered, it will generally look much different than the wireframe you're staring at by pressing your face against the monitor. It's more important to get the big picture correct than every vertex movement tweaked perfectly (there are better secondary deformers like corrective blend shapes to take care of this).

Keeping the previous principles in mind, I have created a guide below to each body part/limb area as best I can in print form. I would highly suggest going through each tutorial video accompanying this book in order to get a better idea of how to apply these principles to any character model you are working on.

8.10.3.5 The Wrist
The wrist is mostly a hinge joint with limited rotation in the lateral plane, in this case the Z-axis. You need to make sure that the skin weights break smoothly from the forearm twist to the wrist joint without losing the volume of the wrist. The wrist is the most common area to lose volume in order to avoid interpenetration, but it's honestly far better to let the geometry intersect and create a cleavage area than it is to make the forearm look oddly skinny. One of the places where you will need to really tweak the position of the joint to get the rotation correct is the wrist (Figure 8.27).

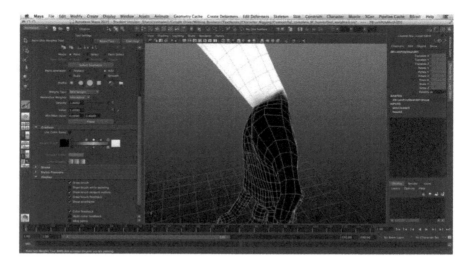

FIGURE 8.27   The wrist weights painted. This joint needs to be changed slightly to improve the position of rotation (see the end of the lesson for a discussion on changing joint positions).

8.10.3.6 The Forearm

The forearm twist is a special area—it really requires at least *two* joints to operate successfully, but currently for brevity's sake I will only be using a single node. Figure 8.28 shows the correct spread of weights to use with the single twist node. It's important to note that you have to spread out the weights well enough to avoid the "candy-wrapper effect," which happens with non-distributed twists, as you can see in Figure 8.29. It's something that dual-quaternion skinning methods are conquering without the need for multiple twist-node rigs, and the fact that DQ weighting and Classic Linear weighting can now be blended is making this less of a problem in a classic character rig. But either way, the skin weight distribution should fan out in both directions toward the wrist and the elbow to spread the twisting action across the forearm vertices. If you have two to four twist nodes, it will still be the same basic principle, just with more joints (see the final lesson in this book).

8.10.3.7 The Elbow

Since the elbow is a hinge joint, you only have to worry about one plane of rotation and that only needs to go from 0 to ~120° (no negative position). The two important parts of the elbow are the inner cleavage area where the bend happens and the point of the elbow in the back. The inner elbow can be seen in Figure 8.23. The back of the elbow, as you can see in Figure 8.28,

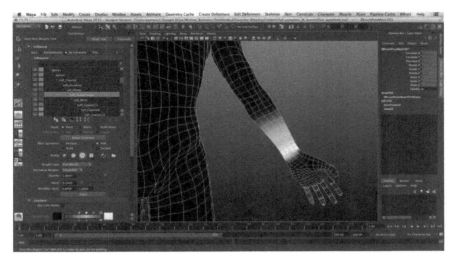

FIGURE 8.28 The spreading of skin weights to facilitate the twisting deformation.

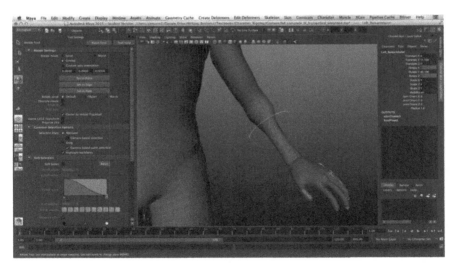

FIGURE 8.29 The "candy-wrapper effect" happens when the twist is too far or not spread out across enough joints.

must maintain its shape and somewhat sharp angle. This means you will have to make sure that the back vertices, as shown in Figure 8.28, will have to have the right balance of weights distributed between the elbow and the Humerus. As you can also see in Figure 8.28, I have spread the influence of the elbow slightly up the triceps area, which will pull the vertices a little bit and simulate the tightening of the skin as the elbow rotates (Figure 8.30).

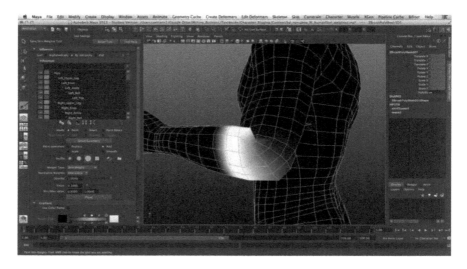

FIGURE 8.30 The back of the elbow, spread evenly and deliberately maintaining a sharp angle.

8.10.3.8 The Humerus

The Humerus is a tricky area, since it's a ball-and-socket joint with two primary axes of rotation in terms of important body mechanics. One thing to remember here is *not* to try and get the twisting aspect of it working with the skin weights, since this part of the joint will be offset onto a twist node eventually. It's still tricky, however, to get the Humerus to work in both the lifting movement (in this case the Z-axis) and the forward/backward movement of the X-axis. It's actually much *easier* when the character is in the A-stance, since the arms are halfway in-between both of these states. The trick is to get the weights working well enough to make the skin look reasonably decent throughout the proper range of motion. So make sure that you aren't overextending the limb when painting weights. It's most likely that you'll run into problems when trying to get it working with both directions and in that case it's best to figure out the most likely range of motion for the character's arms (in this case let's assume they will be walking, running, or holding a gun) and favor *that* range of motion over the other (Figures 8.31 through 8.33).

8.10.4 Step 4: The Clavicle/Humerus/Upper Spine

The Clavicle area is a special area for weighting. If you look at Figure 8.27, you can see how this particular model is weighted in order to get the best results for the Clavicle area. This is an area where we need to spread the

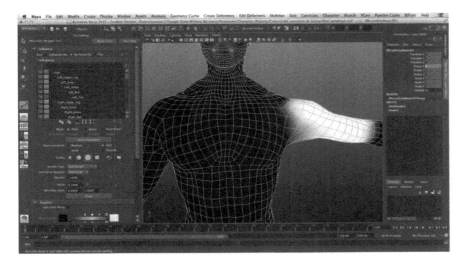

FIGURE 8.31 The lifting of the Humerus in the Z-axis.

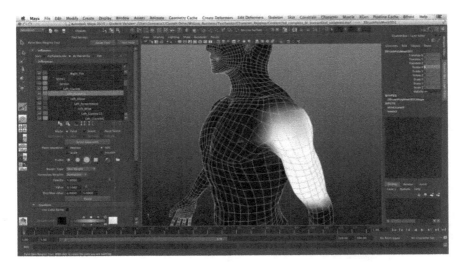

FIGURE 8.32 The back-and-forth movement of the Humerus in the X-axis.

weights across three to four joints, including the Humerus, upper spine, and Clavicle joint. The trick is to rotate the Clavicle in the Z-axis (or whatever axis lifts it) slightly and paint the weights accordingly. As you can see, lifting the Clavicle will also lift the arm, and you can see where you need to paint the weights in order to make a realistic representation of the skinned action (Figure 8.34).

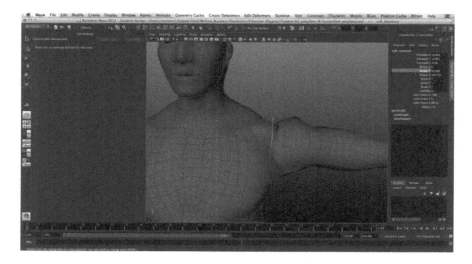

FIGURE 8.33 The twisting motion of the Humerus—ouch! See why we need some other way of getting this twist to happen? We don't want to twist the Humerus itself, but only deduce the twisting action thereof and apply it to some twist nodes down the chain.

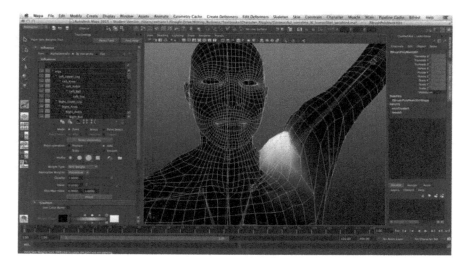

FIGURE 8.34 The weighting of the Clavicle. There will be a lot of tweaking between the Clavicle, upper spine, and Humerus.

8.10.4.1 The Spine

The root, Spine 1, and Spine 2 weights should be spread out enough to control the three axes of movement in a smooth manner, but still applied to maintain the "wrinkle" in the bending forward and back that the character will be doing. The root and upper spine are "solid movement" areas in which the bone structure keeps the area very stiff, but the middle is the "soft movement" area, where there can be smoothed weights and some loss of volume. It's hard to get all three axes of rotation to look perfect with only three joints, but if you spread the weights out evenly from the middle spine node plus "break" the weight values in the wrinkle areas of the belly, you can get good results. I try to use the entire edge loops here to tweak values up and down, creating a consistent appearance when animated (Figures 8.35 through 8.40).

8.10.4.2 The Head and Neck

The head and neck are very similar to the spine and waist—the joints need to rotate in all three planes, but some are more important than others. The down and up movement are the most important, with the twisting being second, and the lean to one side being the last. This is because the head rotates up and down far more often than it leans or twists and with a greater range of motion as well. The neck and head joints work together in the poses in Figures 8.41 through 8.44, where the head usually rotates about 25% more than the neck in any pose.

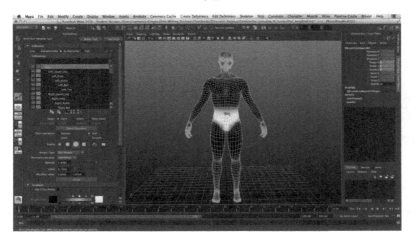

FIGURE 8.35 The root/hips joint weights—notice how they look, like superman's costume a little? This is a good visual guideline for your weighting.

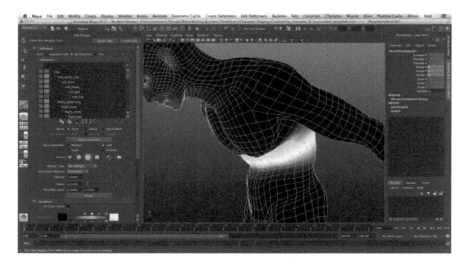

FIGURE 8.36 Bending over at the waist. Make sure the weights are evenly spread between the middle spine and the root and upper spine.

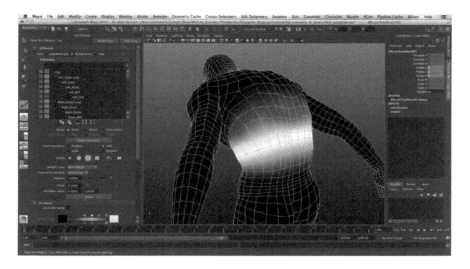

FIGURE 8.37 Bending over at the waist from behind. Notice that there is skin expansion when the vertices stretch and compression when they fold together.

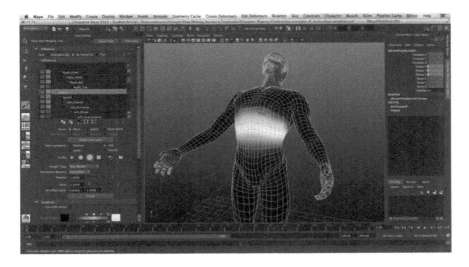

FIGURE 8.38   Bending over backward.

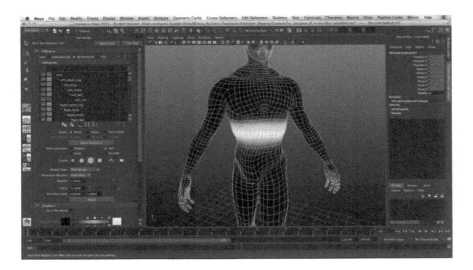

FIGURE 8.39   Do the twist.

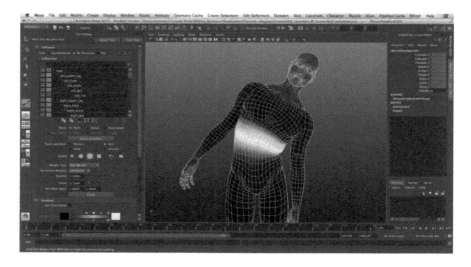

FIGURE 8.40   Leaning to one side.

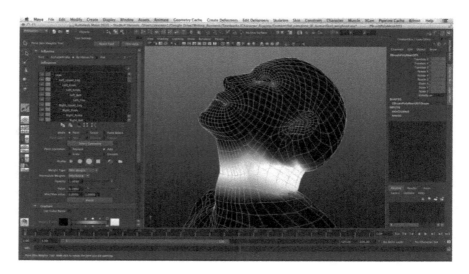

FIGURE 8.41   The head, tilted back, and the skin weights as they should appear on the neck.

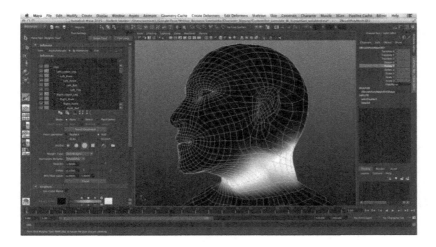

FIGURE 8.42   The head and neck bent backward.

FIGURE 8.43   The head and neck twisted.

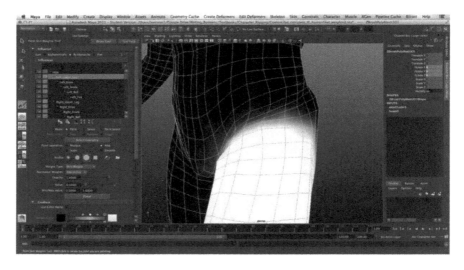

FIGURE 8.44   The head and neck leaning to the side.

8.10.4.3 The Leg

The upper leg, or Femur joint, is similar to the Humerus, but with a much smaller range of motion. As you can see in Figure 8.45, the crease of the hip is where the cleavage of skin occurs. You won't see much inside this crease, but you want the stretch of the opposite direction to be even and well weighted. Where the crease is, it's better to let the leg interpenetrate a little than try to smooth it out. You can see the outer hip in Figure 8.46,

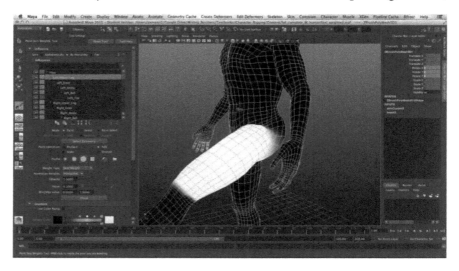

FIGURE 8.45   Weighting at the crease of the hip.

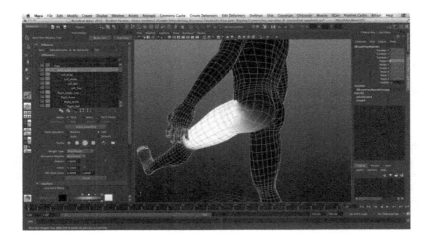

FIGURE 8.46   Weighting on the side of the leg.

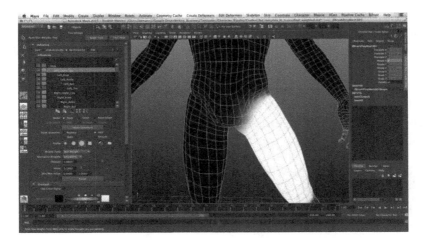

FIGURE 8.47   Weighting from behind, on the butt area.

where the weights are painted to spread the forward rotation across the vertex-sparse area. Figure 8.47 shows the back end of the butt area as it appears when the leg is rotated forward. It is extremely important to maintain volume in the butt! There's nothing like a flat character butt to indicate a poor job of skin weighting. The secondary action of the Femur is to move laterally, as in Figure 8.48, where you can see the hip move outward. Keep in mind that this position is far less common than the upward rotation on the Z-axis (in this case), and the weights should be done for the more common range of motion *first* and take precedence.

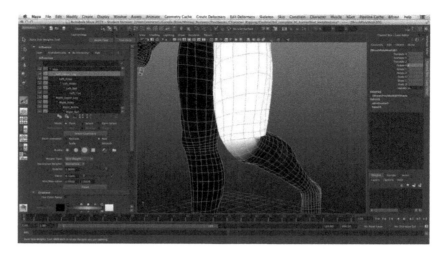

FIGURE 8.48 The lateral movement of the hip and the crotch area.

8.10.4.4 The Knee

The knee, much like the elbow, is a simple area to work on since it is a hinge joint with only one direction of rotation. The front of the knee, as you can see in Figure 8.49, should maintain volume and have a good blended area between the bottom of the quadriceps and the middle part of the knee. This simulates the stretchiness of the skin. In Figure 8.50, you can see the back of the knee, where we have the cleavage point and the thick part of

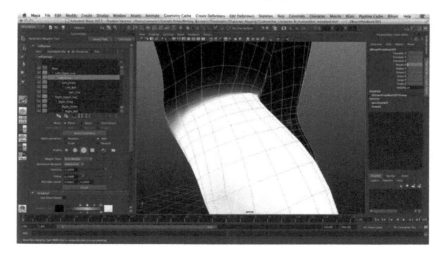

FIGURE 8.49 The knee from the front, bent at 70°, and the skin weights have been blended from the lower quad to the lower part of the knee.

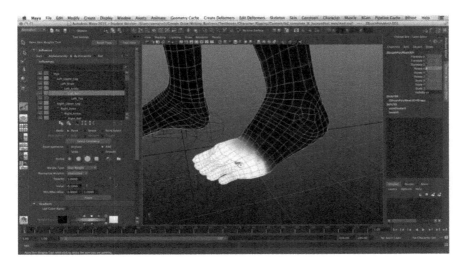

FIGURE 8.50   The back of the knee, where the cleavage occurs.

the calf muscle folding into the skin behind the knee. Interpenetration is just fine here, and even expected, as long as you don't make the shape of the calf lose volume by trying to avoid it.

8.10.4.5 The Ankle and Ball

The ankle actually does move in three axes; however, the range of movement is extremely limited except in the main axis (the World X-axis if you are following the joint orients). Since this is the most important axis of movement, you should always paint weights for it first. The ankle is usually one of the easier areas to paint weights for, due to this very limited range, as you can see in Figure 8.51. The ball of the foot doesn't usually rotate by itself, but is rotated *around* by the ankle; besides it still needs to bend properly with a nice crease in the top and bottom, on a very limited range.

8.10.4.6 The Fingers

With the exception of the "first" knuckles and the thumb, the fingers are identical to the elbow joint! Just approach them in the same manner and you should be fine. The top knuckles operate just like the wrist, in that they have some very limited lateral motion that should be addressed, especially when blending the webbing between the fingers. The webbing will have some partial values from each top knuckle joint on either side (Figures 8.52 through 8.54).

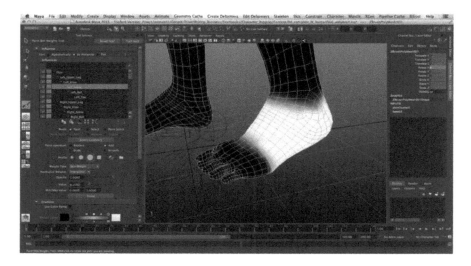

FIGURE 8.51 The weighting of the ankle.

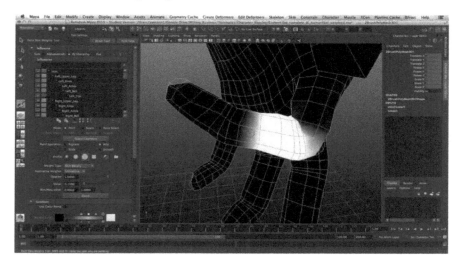

FIGURE 8.52 The weighting of the ball. Make sure it's nice and even on the ground plane!

Congratulations! You now have a completed bind that should deform well with animation data. Getting this part done is not a simple feat! It often takes a rigger weeks to perfect and tweak the skin weights as well as they can. Indeed, it's one of the most challenging and tedious aspects of rigging, but a well-crafted character with good skin weights will add

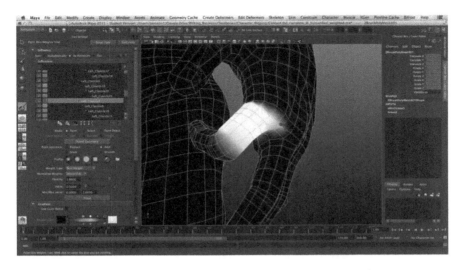

FIGURE 8.53 Knuckles are a lot like elbows! Just on your hands.

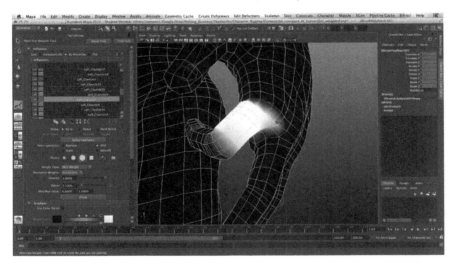

FIGURE 8.54 Blend the top knuckle weight values in the webbing of the fingers.

a lot to the final product. Importing an animation and applying it to the character is a really good way to put it through the paces of deformation and determine where exactly it *isn't* working so that you can continue to tweak the weights in problem areas. Don't stress *too* much about getting those minuscule vertex weights working though! We can adjust those in the secondary deformation phase with corrective blend shapes.

8.10.4.7 Adjusting the Joints after Weighting

One thing that you will need to do often as a character rigger is to determine the optimal placement for your joints for each skeleton/skin. Oftentimes, in large pipelines, the animation skeleton or the primary joints are set in stone, due to technical constraints. But if you are able to change the positions of the important joints, then you should explore minor tweaks to the position in space.

It may seem to be nitpicky at first, but as you work with multiple skin weight solutions you will find that even minor tweaks in the position of the joint can yield significant improvements in the appearance of the skin weighting. The Move Skinned Joints Tool has been discussed previously in this book and is a good tool to use in assisting you to previsualize what a difference in the position of the joint would do to the skinning model— but it's a little dangerous in a way because it can mess up your joint orients and it's not completely mirror friendly if you have mirrored your joints with "behavior," which flips the primary axis of the joint. But for repositioning your joints on a skinned mesh and testing the results of those altered positions, it works fine. Once you have determined the optimal position for each joint in your skeleton, you will have to mirror the joints again, rebind the model, and reapply the weights. In order to preserve the skin weight information you will have to export the skin weight maps, which will depend on UVs being present on the model. You can then reimport them after rebinding your model to the skeleton, but make sure that all the names are the same from the original skeleton or there might be issues. Alternately, there are some vertex-based skin weight export plugins out there as well.

CHAPTER 9

Relationships

9.1 HOW DO YOU MAKE RELATIONSHIPS BETWEEN ONE NODE AND ANOTHER?

Relationships in 3D are the heart of what "rigging" really stands for. It is the third pillar of character rigging (after kinematics and deformation). We create relationships between one node and another in order to generate secondary deformation and a multitude of tasks that require something to happen based on certain factors or inputs. It's in essence a sort of visual programming, where you connect one thing to another based on parameters and mathematical functions. Although in my first book, *Essential Skills in 3D Modeling, Rendering, and Animation*, I stayed away from math completely, in this case we are going to have to start using and understanding basic aspects of math in order to get certain things working properly. The good news is that most of it is done visually, and not with equations, with the exception of expressions.

9.2 WHY DO YOU NEED TO MAKE RELATIONSHIPS BETWEEN ONE NODE AND ANOTHER?

Relationships allow you to drive the action of one thing from the parameters of another. This is invaluable in rigging because we often need to control the movement of certain joints with others, such as the twist nodes in an upper arm (which we'll explore in one of the lessons). It can also provide a structure for controlling certain aspects of the skeleton that will be animated by the animator like a marionette, where all the controls of a single limb are condensed into one node, simplifying the

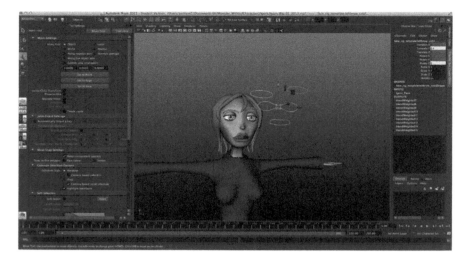

FIGURE 9.1   (**See color insert.**) The floating curves are used to control the many parts of the face joints.

animation process. In order to create these marionette-like controls, you must be able to connect certain aspects of nodes to others. Face rigs are also a place where relationships between several nodes are created to allow the animator to set keyframes on facial expressions, instead of directly onto the joints themselves. The joints have behaviors that are controlled by the sliders on the face rig, which are in turn controlled by the animator and keyframes. We use various relationships to connect the two together. Figure 9.1 shows a very simple facial rig that controls a low-poly character. The floating elements resemble a face, and when they are moved in a 2D plane they trigger movements of the character's facial features.

9.3 WHAT ARE CONSTRAINTS AND WHAT DO WE USE THEM FOR?

Constraints are an almost universal method in 3D programs to connect the transform of one object to another. Almost every 3D package has some forms of constraints, although they sometimes go under different names. There are several "exotic" constraints available in Maya, but the primary ones we will be exploring are Point, Orient, Aim, Parent, and Pole Vector. These are the most commonly used constraints in any program.

A constraint works by creating a *target* object, which is the constraining object to the constrained object. The transforms of the target are fed into the constrained object. You are allowed to have multiple targets, which will all have a weight value so that you can blend them together. So it is possible to have several objects affecting the constrained objects, as well as animating the weight values in order to switch influences in the middle of an animation. The application of a constraint is somewhat non-intuitive if you're used to parenting objects since it works in reverse of that (in a fashion). When you want to constrain one object to another, you first select the *target* object, then select the *object to be constrained*, then create the constraint. This is the opposite of parenting one object to another, in which you select the child, then the parent (although these are two different processes with two different results). It's very common to create your constraints backward by accident, and my students do this all the time. The constraint itself is a node, which gets parented underneath the constrained object, and you can delete the node to remove it (or choose the menu item constraint > remove) (Figures 9.2 and 9.3).

A Point Constraint will constrain the X, Y, or Z translation of one object to another. You can choose only one axis, or all three at once. Figure 9.4 shows the option box of the point constraint. Maintain offset is an option that will keep the constrained object in its current position, but any movement of the target object will also move the constrained object.

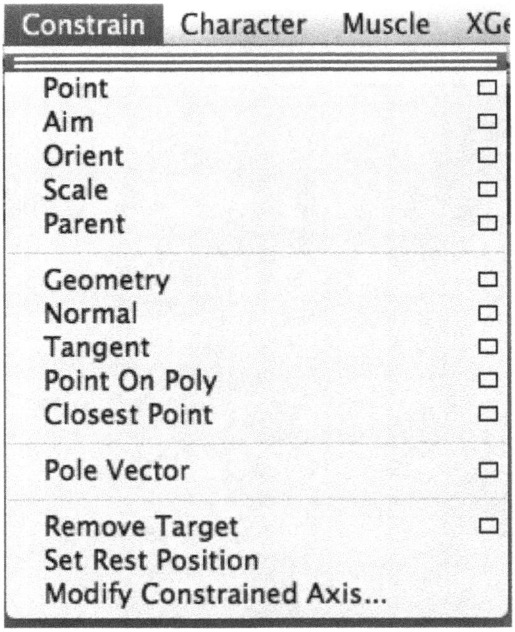

FIGURE 9.2 The constraint menu.

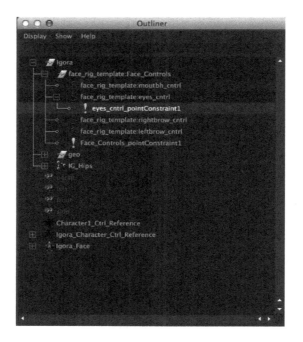

FIGURE 9.3 The constraint is an actual node, parented underneath the constrained object.

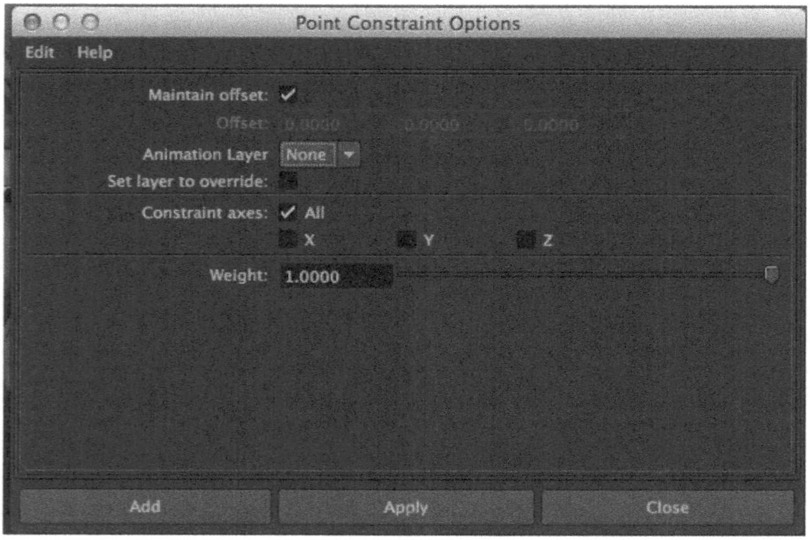

FIGURE 9.4 The Point constraint options.

If this is *not* checked, the local position values of the constrained object will immediately assume the local position values of the target object, which will effectively put the constrained object right on top of the target object. Sometimes this is desirable, but more often than not you want to keep maintain offset on. This will make the constrained object move *with* the target object, but from its original position. The layer options here are for creating an extra animation layer and an override so that you can turn it off without removing the constraint. The weight value, from 0 to 1, will affect how much influence a target has on the constrained movement—if there are multiple targets, this value will change how much influence it has from 0% to 100%. But if there is only a single target, this value is either zero, or has no influence, and any number higher than zero will have 100% influence.

An Orient Constraint will constrain the Euler XYZ rotational values from one object to another, based on the *constrained* object's pivot point. This means that, when you rotate the target object, the constrained object will also rotate, but around its own pivot, and not the target object's pivot. The options for an Orient Constraint are identical to the Point Constraint.

An Aim Constraint, often called a "look-at" constraint in other software packages, is a special kind of constraint. It will constrain the *rotation* of the constrained object to the *translation* of the target object. It does this by using a Vector, which essentially draws a straight line from the pivot of the constrained object to the target object, and then rotates the constrained object in order to maintain that line, effectively looking at the target. An aim constraint has a special set of parameters upon creating that control how it evaluates. Figure 9.5 shows these parameters. The Aim Vector is the axis upon which the constrained object will look at the target object. The Up Vector determines which way is "up" to the constrained object, and the World Up type determines which direction is the global up for the constraint, which if the object is inside a hierarchy can make the object's up be the world up to avoid flipping. Generally, we want these two to be the same in simple aim constraint setups, but when there are more advanced elements involved, we will need to edit the world up and up vector to be specific to our needs. This is often the case when creating constraints based on joints that have been oriented, since they have totally different local rotational alignments from the World (Figure 9.6).

A Parent Constraint is very similar to a Point and Orient Constraint, but with one vital difference—the constrained object gets its transform offset from the *target* object's pivot! This allows it to behave as if it is

FIGURE 9.5   Parameters for an Aim Constraint.

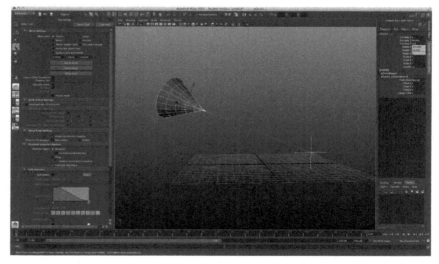

FIGURE 9.6   A simple aim constraint in action, using the parameters from Figure 9.5.

parented, but not to be inside the hierarchy, which is very convenient in certain circumstances, especially when you want to mimic the behavior of a hierarchy, *but* you need to turn it off or swap controlling elements, which you cannot do with a hierarchy. So, in effect, the Parent Constraint allows you to change which object is the Parent (or acting Parent) for various purposes. One thing to note about *all* constraints is that they override any transforms of the constrained object, which means that *unlike* a hierarchical relationship you can't edit their controlled transforms anymore—those will now be determined by the constraint.

Pole Vector Constraints are set to work specifically with a Pole Vector of a Rotate-Plane Inverse Kinematics (IK) Chain. This acts as a very specific aim constraint, where the Pole Vector of an IK chain will rotate based on an object's world space position. This is used mostly in determining the "twist" action of a Humerus or Femur joint area, where the ball-and-socket joints can be turned in either direction. The Pole Vector can be independently edited on the IK handle, but it's much easier and handy to have a node that can have its positions animated using a position transform.

There are other constraints available, as you can see, but they are slightly more advanced, technically specific, and out of the scope of this book. Constraints are the go-to techniques for creating simple relationships between the transform of one object and another, and an invaluable part of rigging. They are limited, however, since they can only make one-to-one relationships between transforms, and lack the ability to customize the value from one object to another. For instance, you can't divide the rotation of one object by a certain number and apply it to another based on a constraint—you have to use something more sophisticated.

9.4 WHAT ARE EXPRESSIONS?

Expressions are mathematical formulae that can be applied to certain channels with a limited set of scripting capabilities in order to generate values based on pure math. Expressions can take multiple values and apply basic math functions to those values, which will be evaluated in a single attribute channel (which can be any attribute channel). They evaluate at run-time, which is to say they're always "on," unless you use a value of time in the equation, which will need to be updated by hitting play on the time shuttle or scrubbing through the frames. Expressions are very easy to write once you get the hang of them, and extremely powerful tools in customizing the relationship from one value to another, although they are often times intimidating to artists who haven't used them. After all, we don't want to do any *math* or *coding*, right? Well, unfortunately in the world of character rigging and setup, aspects of code and math become unavoidable. I tend to think of this as objective-based learning, where the need to create a specific relationship leads us to use expressions in order to make that happen.

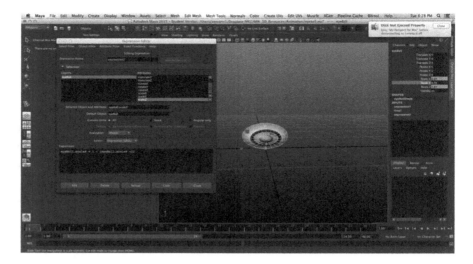

FIGURE 9.7 **(See color insert.)** The squishy ball, now automated with an expression. I guess we have to do some math after all.

In Figure 9.7, I have our old "squishy ball" from the lesson in my previous book, *Essential Skills in 3D Modeling, Rendering, and Animation*. In order to create volume-based scaling, I have been scaling this ball from a pivot point at the bottom, and ensuring that volume is maintained by removing the same amount of scale from the X and Z axes as I add to the Y-axis, and vice versa. This maintains a volume in the object to make it appear to squish and stretch, like a pliant material. Since I have a consistent mathematical relationship happening, it's a perfect place for an expression!

All I have to do for this setup is create an expression which says that the Scale X and Z of the ball are inversely proportionate to the Scale of the Y value. The mathematical formula I use for this is: Scale X = 1—(Scale Y – 1). This formula, used for both the X and Z scale axes will create volume retention in the eyeball, based on the scale of the Y-axis. In Maya, an expression is entered in the appropriate channel in the Expression Editor. Expressions are nice because you can use any channel in your scene as a variable, including special ones like Time, which will change as the integer time value changes. So with expressions, we can have a complex equation full of multiple variables that can be connected to any channel in your scene. Expressions are great for complex mathematical relationships, and they can easily be translated into game code or scripted in some type of IDE game development kit like Unity3D or Unreal. Expressions really are some of the most flexible ways of creating a relationship between one channel and another; however, they require a lot of math and some coding skills, and oftentimes a complex relationship can be created with less technical knowledge or mathematical background. Expressions can use simple logic with "if" and "else" statements, which makes it fairly powerful for a lot of tasks that would otherwise be difficult to do.

One limitation of an expression is that only a single expression can drive a single channel at once, as opposed to other relationship methods that can blend multiple inputs, like Constraints or Driven Keys.

9.5 WHAT ARE MATH NODES?

Maya math nodes are pre-fab mathematical computations that were originally intended to control materials and shading networks, but can have a great amount of use in the arena of character rigging. They work by connecting inputs and outputs in the Hypergraph, or Maya's new Node Editor. There are too many of these to go into detail about the function of each one, but there is a smaller set that are used frequently in character setup, which I will go over. Figure 9.8 illustrates these nodes, arranged in the Hypershade. In order to use these nodes, one must create them from the Hypershade and then open either the Hypergraph or

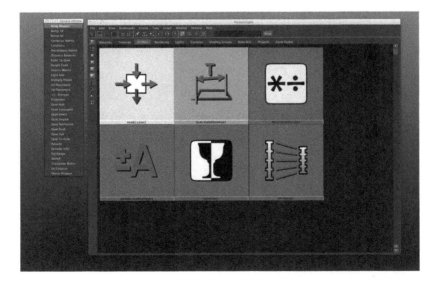

FIGURE 9.8 **(See color insert.)** Some math utility nodes that are frequently useful in character rigging.

Node Editor to make the connections between one node and another. You can also edit the parameters of each in the attribute editor.

A Condition is a node that takes two terms and compares them. You can choose which operator you want: less than, greater than, equal to, less than or equal to, or greater than or equal to. The output value (in this case a float value) is then sent to another channel if the condition is true or false. You can control a lot of aspects of a character with this node, based on a single value or a set of values (Figure 9.9).

A Distance Between node is a node that, given two Vector 3 values, ostensibly taken from two points or transforms in 3D space, will output the distance between them. This is really useful if you need to do something based on the distance one object is from another one.

The Multiple/Divide and Plus/Minus/Average nodes are useful for doing basic arithmetic to multiple values. They work the same as the rest of the nodes, in which you will connect one object in your scene to another via the node you create using the Node Editor.

Reverse is a node that will negate any value you give it, which is very useful in flipping joint values, pole vectors, or any other aspect of a joint rotation that might need to be reversed in certain cases.

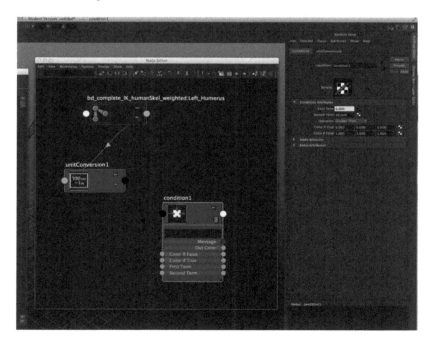

FIGURE 9.9 The Node editor, with connections.

Set Range is a very nice and simple way of doing what would otherwise be a complex calculation. It allows you to cast one range of values into another range of values. This can be done with some calculative work in the Expression Editor, but it's much easier to do in the math node, since all you have to do is plug in the old min and old max, and the new min and new max, and the output value will automatically update with the input value. In this way you can recast certain number ranges to values between 0 and 1, which is called normalizing. This is especially useful in setting up corrective blend shapes, since the slider value of a blend shape goes from 0 to 1, and oftentimes they are based on joint rotations, which are values somewhere between 0 and 360.

9.6 WHAT ARE DRIVEN KEYS?

Driven keys are the last, but most unique and important relationship method when setting up a character. Driven keys are extremely flexible in ways the other methods of relationships are not, and they allow multiple inputs per channel! Driven keys also offer the artist, or nontechnical person, an easy way to quickly create customized relationships between one object and another with a relatively large amount of flexibility in how that relationship evaluates.

A Driven Key, simply stated, is a manipulation of the concept of an animation and keyframing. Instead of saving a value at a position in time (known as a keyframe), a Driven Key saves a value for *another value*. So it acts much as an animation curve, but the X-axis (horizontal) is now the driving value instead of time. The *driving* value is the channel from which the *driven* value derives its information. So when the driving value is at a certain place, the driven value is at a certain place, but the interpolation between those two points of reference is controlled by the motion graph curve, just like an animation. In Figure 9.10 you can see the graph curve depiction of this relationship. It *looks* like a time-based relationship, but in fact it's a *value*-based relationship. In this case, we have a custom slider that goes from 0 to 1, which controls the opening of the jaw bone of a fish model. When the slider value is at 1, we want the fish jaw to be open. When it is at 0, we want it to be closed.

Driven keys can be connected to multiple outputs, and each driven channel can have multiple inputs. This means that a single channel can have several driving values that will influence its final value, which will be averaged based on the drivers. This is a distinct advantage for rigging needs like face animation rigs, which require that a rigging element

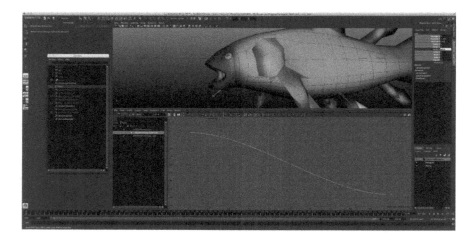

FIGURE 9.10 **(See color insert.)** The relationship of a driven key animation curve. The fish jaw opening is controlled by the interpolation of the values between the keys of the attribute slider.

be controlled by more than one channel at once. Driven keys also offer the nontechnical artist a quick and visual approach to making relationships between one object and another. Another nice feature is the editing of tangents in the graph editor to create acceleration and deceleration curves based on the relationship, which is only possible with this type of relationship.

9.7 WHAT'S THE BEST METHOD OF GENERATING A RELATIONSHIP? WHAT ARE THE DIFFERENCES BETWEEN ONE METHOD AND ANOTHER?

What method of rigging you use is often driven by what your immediate need is, and what your intended output is. If you are only working in Maya, then everything is at your disposal. But if you're going out to a game engine like Unity3D or Unreal, then the options are much smaller—in fact you will most likely not be able to use driven keys, math nodes, or even expressions and constraints natively.

Generally speaking, I tend to use expressions when there is a definitive mathematical relationship I can easily write out as an equation. Math nodes can do similar things, but for most of those things I use an expression unless I need a specific feature like a distance between measurement. Constraints are best used when you need to create a transform-based relationship between one object and another—indeed that's what they're there for! Certainly you could do this with another type of relationship (especially a constraint), but it wouldn't be nearly as easy to do.

Driven keys are great tools for rigging, and I generally use them for complex actions and face rigs, where I need multiple inputs to go into a single channel. They are flexible, fast to set up, easy to edit, and offer a vast amount of control over the end result.

In conclusion, the ability to create relationships between one object and another is the primary role of the technical character artist. Musculatures, high-end deformation, and the complex mechanics of an organic body demand that multiple techniques be used to ensure that these all work in harmony. Rigging anything requires knowledge of the *full* set of tools available to connect one action of a rig to another. Learning these tools and how to use them in what situations is a matter of experience and repetition. Once you have learned how to set up the mechanics of something once, that particular set of relationships will often help you with a different problem.

9.8 LESSON 1: THE REVERSE FOOT

OK, now that we have a skeleton and a mesh that are bound and weighted, we need to get to the rigging! What does that entail? Well, every character rig is different, and often tailored to the exact needs of the person intending to use it and the place where the finished product will be going in the end. But we will be rigging our character for the specific purpose of having an animator take the completed character and animate it. This means we need very specific things set up to assist in that process. The next several lessons will use our relationship types, as discussed previously, along with some deformers and IK adjustments to generate a comprehensive (but basic) human control set for our animator.

Our first order of business is to set up a foot rig that will make planting and rolling the foot an easy task. There are multiple ways of doing this, but the Reverse Foot setup is the most universally used, and in my opinion the easiest. It consists of three distinct steps: making the IK handles, creating the reverse foot structure, and then parenting the IK handles under the correct nodes.

9.8.1 Step 1: Create the IK Handles

We will begin by creating a Rotate-Plane IK Handle from the hip to the ankle. Make sure that your knee joint has the unneeded rotation degrees of freedom turned off, as you can see in Figure 9.11, *before* you create the

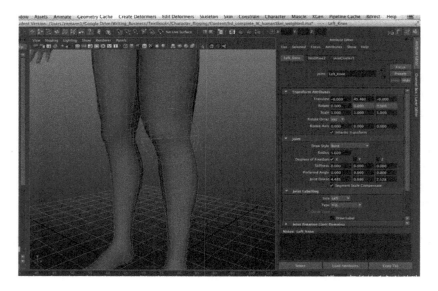

FIGURE 9.11   I have turned off the degrees of freedom for all but the X-axis here, so that the knee bends only on that axis.

IK handle. Also if need be, make sure the preferred angle is set (which will only matter if your leg is unflexed and the knee not bent in the stance pose). Then we will create IK handle from the Ankle to the Ball joints, and then the Ball to the Toe joint. These two-joint IK chains are the simplest way to create translation points that will control the rotation of the joints while they are using IK. These three IK handles are essential in making sure that the foot "plants" and stays in place when the rest of the body is moving around it. Using the "sticky" option will keep the IK handle in place even without any animation data on it. If this is turned off, the IK handle will move with the Forward Kinematics (FK) joints until it has been given a keyframe. Figure 9.12 illustrates the three IK handles on the foot.

9.8.2 Step 2: Creating the Reverse Foot Structure

In creating the Reverse Foot structure, we can use any type of node we want—joints, polygons, locators, or empty groups. It doesn't really matter here since we just need a set of transforms underneath which to put our IK handles (or constrain them). What IS important is the hierarchical order of the nodes—they will be in reverse order of the regular foot! I am going to use joints, because it's the best way to illustrate the hierarchy in a single image, due to the way Maya draws the joints, so you can see which is the parent and which is the child. I will create four joints here: RV Heel,

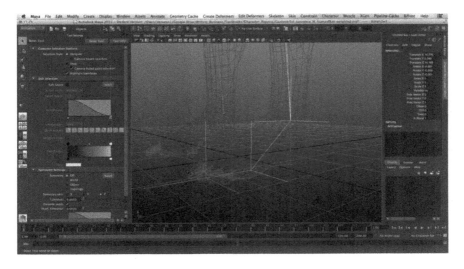

FIGURE 9.12   The three IK handles necessary for the rolling action of the foot.

RV Toe, RV Ball, and RV Ankle. The "RV" stands for "reverse foot" so neither of us get confused about which is which! The RV Toe, RV Ball, and RV Ankle are snapped in position at the same place where their regular foot joints exist, and the RV Heel is a duplicate of the RV Ankle, but set to a Y-value of 0, so that it's flush with the ground plane.

In Figure 9.13 you can see the hierarchical order of the joints I have created: Heel > Toe > Ball > Ankle. The heel joint is there to simulate the point of contact with the ground, which is lacking if we just rotate the foot from the ankle. The foot, when contacting the ground, doesn't so much rotate *from* the ankle as the leg rotates *around* the ankle. But the point of contact here is really either the ball, or the heel (or both). So we are constructing a reverse hierarchy to create that action.

9.8.3 Step 3: Parenting the IK Handles

Now we must correspond the IK handles of the regular foot joints to the transforms of the Reverse Foot joints. There are multiple ways of doing this. We could either use constraints or we could just parent the IK handles under the RV foot joints. For the sake of making things more succinct, I will be parenting the IK handles although constraints can often be slightly more stabile since it does not involve putting the IK handles inside a transform hierarchy where they must inherit transforms (which *can* cause problems in some instances but here it seems to not be an issue).

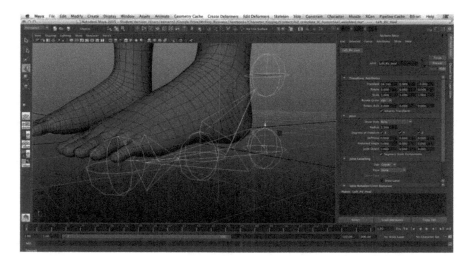

FIGURE 9.13 **(See color insert.)** This is the reverse foot skeleton. Notice that it's not a part of the base skeleton. It's a whole separate thing that is used as a rigging element. Also notice that it has been moved slightly off to the side so that it is visible. Normally, it would be right on top of the regular foot joints.

It's a pretty simple match-up. Parent the Ankle IK handle to the RV Ankle joint, parent the Ball IK handle to the RV Ball joint, and parent the Toe IK handle to the RV Toe joint. Now the RV heel joint will control the entire foot, making it possible to rotate the entire structure left, right, or up and down from that transform. Rotating the RV Ball will lift the heel off from the ground while keeping the ball flat, which will generate the "rolling" foot action, which occurs while we are walking or running. Rotating the RV Toe will allow you to swivel the foot on the ball to perform complex actions like dancing or stomping out a cigarette. In order to create an extra node that allows you to rotate the entire foot from the ankle pivot, you can Group the RV Heel and place the pivot of this group at the ankle joint. This adds the extra option of rotating the entire foot from the pivot of the ankle instead of the heel, which might be useful in actions like swimming, flying, or doing Pilates (wait, our character does Pilates?) (Figures 9.14 through 9.17).

9.9 LESSON 2: THE POLE VECTOR

Pole Vectors are tricky animals. As a rigger you will often have to tinker with them and set them up so that the animator will be able to properly animate specific parts of the body, most often being the arm, and less often the legs.

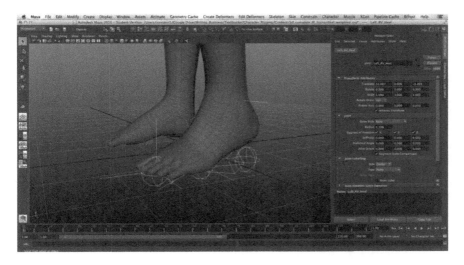

FIGURE 9.14 The RV Ball will roll the ankle around the ball.

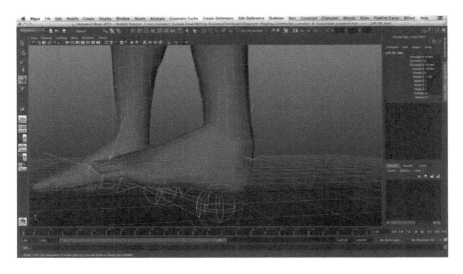

FIGURE 9.15 The heel lifts up from the ground. How else are you going to tap your foot to music?

A Pole Vector is the plane upon which the IK chain solves. There's a lot of math stuff going on there—but the simplest explanation of this pole vector is that it provides the IK chain with the proper twist rotation value to determine how that chain rotates. In terms of the arm IK setup, it means which plane the elbow is pointing. Figure 9.14 shows a typical IK arm setup, where the position of the IK handle, and thus the end effector,

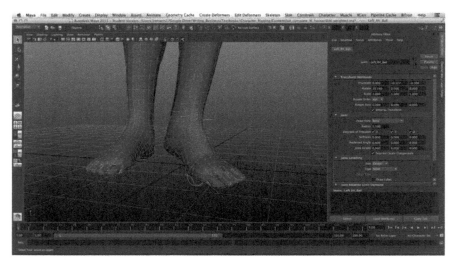

FIGURE 9.16   The Reverse Foot setup is good for things like this—imagine trying to stomp out a cigarette without this rig!

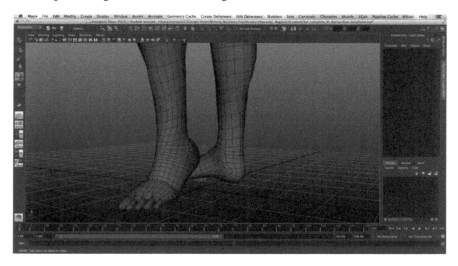

FIGURE 9.17   Ballet, anyone?

is slightly forward of the character. Now the thing is, since the IK solution is rotating the joints of the elbow and the Humerus/upper arm based on the position of the effector, there is more than one valid solution, depending on how you rotate the Humerus on its spin axis! In this case our spin axis is the Y-axis of the joint. Figure 9.15 shows you how this IK solution looks with a different plane—both solutions are correct, but they have drastically different appearances (Figures 9.18 and 9.19).

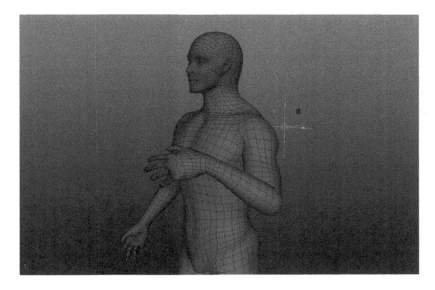

FIGURE 9.18   The IK solution as the wrist is in front of the character.

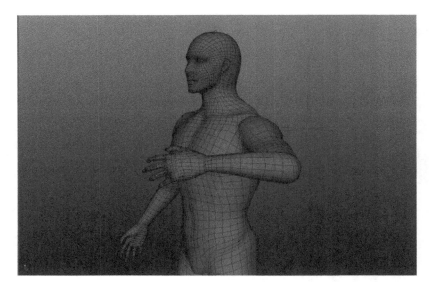

FIGURE 9.19   The IK solution as the Pole Vector is adjusted. The wrist is still in the same position, but the arm is in a totally different position!

So how do we go about changing that plane of the arm and point our elbow in a certain direction? Well that's where the Pole Vector comes in. The Pole Vector determines this by aiming at a point in space, which then changes the plane based on that aim. The Pole Vector transform can either be edited directly or set up with a Pole Vector Constraint (the typical way to handle this). A Pole Vector Constraint uses some kind of object to use the translate position to represent the position of the Pole Vector. Once we create the object and constraint, we can animate it in order to adjust the Pole Vector as we animate the character. So let's set this up!

We start with our character arm IK, as set up in Chapter 6, Lesson 1. We have a Rotate Plane IK handle from the Humerus to the Forearm Twist, as previously set up, shown in Figure 9.20. Now we need to create and set up our pole vector constraint object.

We will use a Locator, which is a Maya "null" object, or just a visual representation of a transform node. Go to Create > Locator and name this "L_PV." Next we will snap the L_PV object to the Clavicle joint using the Point Snap (v is the shortcut key here) and then move the position of the Locator back 20 units in the Z, as you see in Figure 9.21. This offset gives the pole vector room to calculate something based on an angle. If the object is too close, the angles don't have as much room to calculate and smaller movements on the constraint axis result in a much more sensitive action.

FIGURE 9.20 The Arm and simple IK setup.

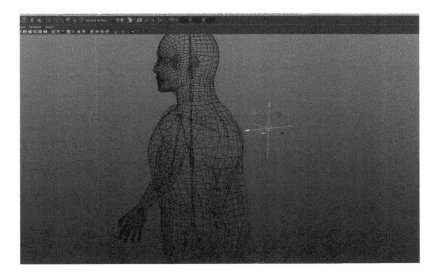

FIGURE 9.21 The L_PV locator placed behind the Clavicle 20 units.

Next, we will parent the L_PV to the Clavicle. This sets it inside the space of the upper body, which will keep the arm from being offset when the torso twists or the Clavicle is rotated. There are several parent spaces you can have the Pole Vector Constraint target in, but I like this one the best because it stays with the upper body, but is independent of the arms.

Now we will select the L_PV object, and then the IK handle controlling the arm and go to Constrain > Pole Vector Constraint (Figure 9.22).

OK, now that you have created the constraint, translating the L_PV object in the Y and X axes will affect the plane that the elbow bends on, which effectively adjusts the Humerus joint rotations. Keyframing this value in an animation will allow the animator control of the position of the wrist *and* the vector the elbow aims. It's a vital component to complex arm animations, although it vastly complicates the animation process by creating a whole new element to coordinate.

There are many more sophisticated and complex ways to set up the pole vector for controlling the plane of rotation on the arm—this is just the simplest!

9.10 LESSON 3: DRIVING HAND POSES WITH DRIVEN KEYS

Driven keys are some of the most powerful rigging tools available in Maya. One of the best applications of this type of relationship is to use it for complex pose sets in hand and face animation. In this lesson,

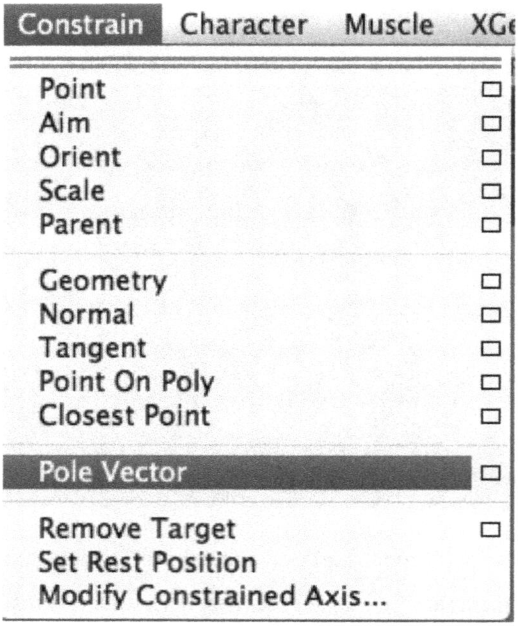

FIGURE 9.22   Create the Pole Vector Constraint.

we will be using a simple set of driven keys to drive a series of hand poses, which would otherwise be very difficult to animate.

In Figure 9.23 you can see the fully articulated hand skeleton, set up for our human model. I have also created a simple NURBS circle and aligned it with the wrist node in order to use it as a "rigging" node, or in some programs a "helper" node. This is just an object we can use to collect our controls for various aspects of the limbs. In this case I have created a Point Constraint from the IK handle controlling the arm to the ArmControl NURBS circle, which will allow me to animate the entire arm through a single object.

The first step is to create the sliders for the hand poses. We will do this by creating custom attributes for our hand poses on the ArmControl node we have created. Creating custom attributes is a great way to set up your own sliders to drive multiple objects in your scene from a single node.

First we select the ArmControl and open the Attribute Editor. Using the pull-down menu, select "attribute" and choose "add attribute," as you can see in Figure 9.24.

Next, we will set up our custom attribute in the attribute creation box, as you can see in Figure 9.25. We will name this attribute L_Point_Pose, which refers to the pointing pose of the hand. Make sure that you are

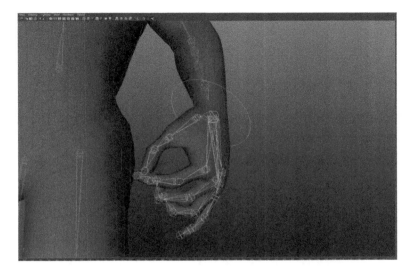

FIGURE 9.23 **(See color insert.)** The articulated hand joints. The NURBS Circle is the rigging node we'll be using to control the arm limb.

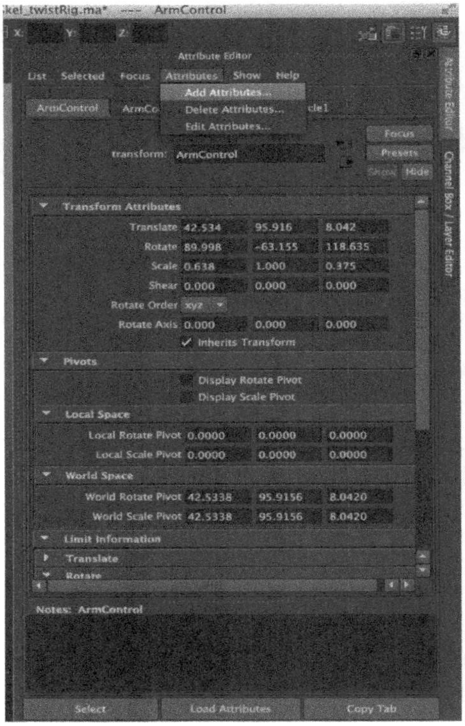

FIGURE 9.24 Creating the custom attribute from the attribute editor.

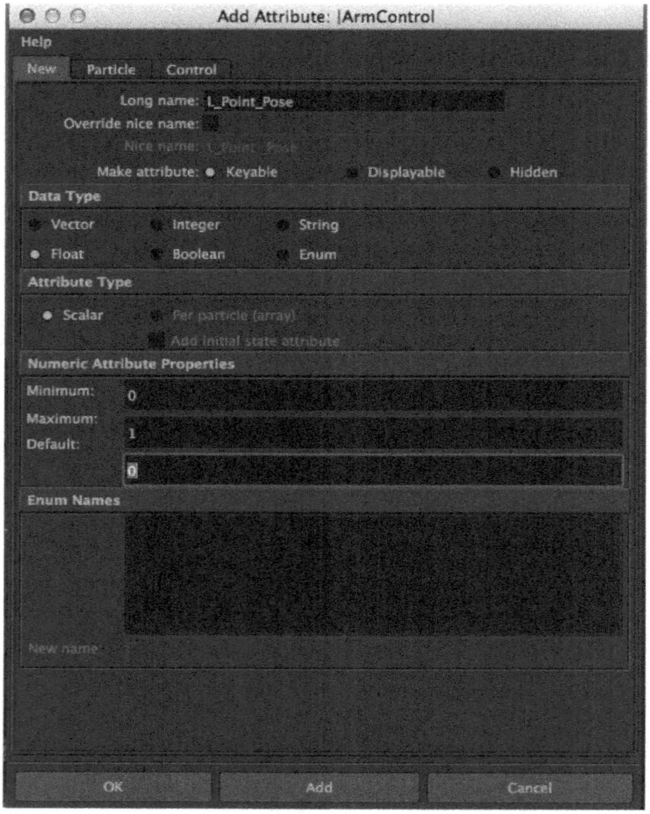

FIGURE 9.25 Setting up the custom attribute.

using a float value and make the minimum value 0 and the maximum value 1. This sets up a slider that goes from the neutral state to the pose being completely on (Figure 9.26).

Now that we have the attribute L_Point_Pose created, we can begin setting up the Driven Keys that will drive the rotation of the hand joints based on the value of this slider. Make sure that you don't have anything selected in Maya, then open the Driven Key Editor by accessing the pull-down menu Animate > Set Driven Key > Set, as you can see in Figure 9.27. This will bring up the Driven Key Editor. Select the ArmControl object and click the Load Driver button at the bottom of the window. This selects the object and channel from which you will be doing the "driving," or the control channel. Next you will select *all* the objects that will be controlled by this channel, which in this case are all the pertinent finger joints. Once you have selected them, load them up into the Driven channels by clicking the Load Driven

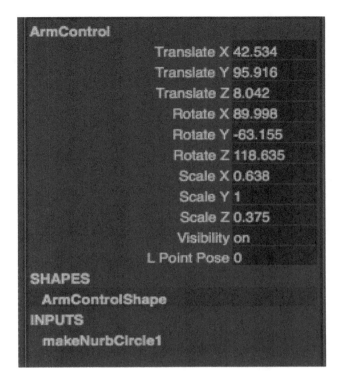

FIGURE 9.26   The attribute we have created in the channel control. It's also in the "extra attributes" section in the Attribute Editor.

button at the bottom of the Driven Key Editor. You will then highlight the L_Point_Pose channel in the Driven Section, and all of the finger joints below as well as their rotate X, Y, and Z axes, as shown in Figure 9.28. You can drive all of these channels at once from a single attribute, which makes it very convenient for setting up complex sets of poses.

Once we have the appropriate channels matched up, we will set a zero key by clicking the Key button. This establishes the state of the driven values at the zero value of the driver channel—this is an important step! Without it we don't know what the neutral, or initial, pose is. Next we will change the driver value, L_Point_Pose, to 1. This indicates that the hand should be completely in the Point Pose. Make sure you don't forget this step, or you could accidentally spend a lot of time posing the hand only to find it snap back to the initial pose!

Now that we have turned the Point Pose "on," we can begin adjusting the joint rotations of the fingers to shape the hand into that pose. This could take a while—make sure you don't close out the Driven Key Editor

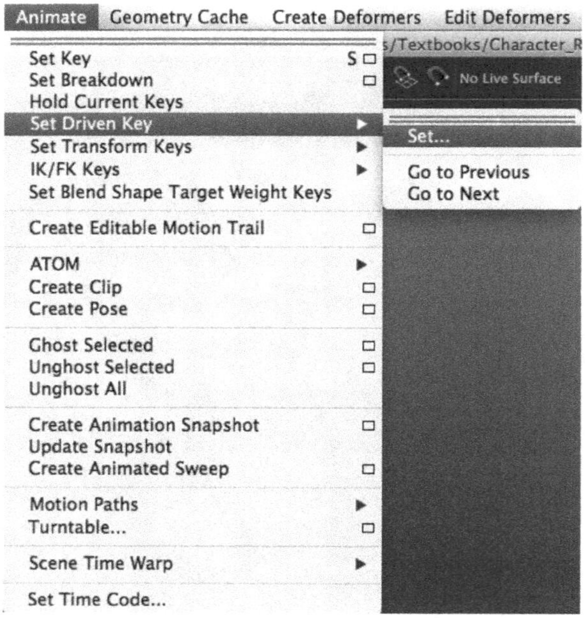

FIGURE 9.27 Opening the Driven Key Editor.

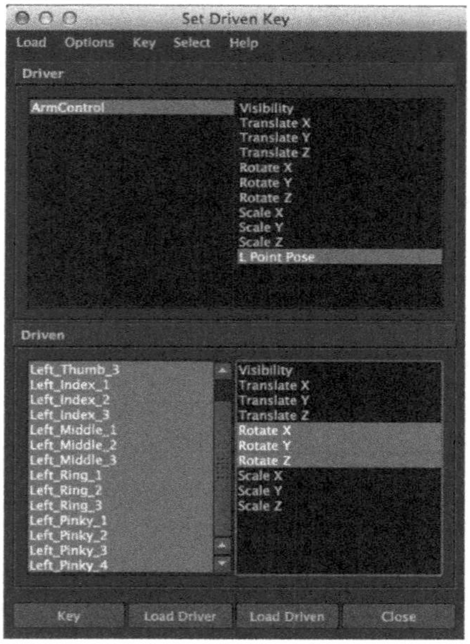

FIGURE 9.28 Selecting the driver channels and the driven channels. You can select only one driver at a time, but you can have that channel drive as many channels at once as your heart desires.

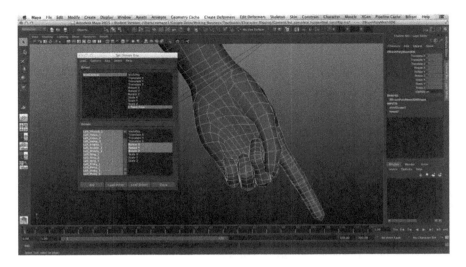

FIGURE 9.29   The finished L_Point_Pose. Now we can quickly transition from neutral to this pose with a single slider. Using the Driven Key relationship can save us a ton of time and energy by rapidly creating a visual connection between one attribute and multiple attributes.

or you'll have to do all that selecting and loading over again (Figure 9.29). Finish adjusting the pose of the fingers to match how you want them, and then click on the Key button again and it will save this pose; transition between it and the neutral when you change the value of the L_Point_Pose attribute!

And that's the whole process! Using this you can create dozens of custom poses, connections, and relationships between on channel and multiple others. It's fast, flexible, simple to use, and doesn't require a degree in algebra to use. Driven Keys are a great way for artists to set up rigs and behaviors in an intuitive fashion. So experiment as much as you like with this technique, since it has a plethora of practical uses.

9.11 LESSON 4: DRIVING CORRECTIVE BLEND SHAPES

Remember all that talk about "secondary deformation"? Well, here's where we get to put it to use! Secondary deformation is based on "correctives," or deformations that allow us to tweak and edit the deformation in certain areas of the body using extra deformers. There are plenty of these in Maya that we can use—muscle deformers, wrap deformers, clusters, etc. But the one that is used more often than others in the game development industry is the *corrective blend shape*, because it's far more universal than the others and is easily carried over into a real-time engine. It's also supported by Unity3D and Unreal engines natively, and a cinch to implement.

Blend shapes, as we have previously learned, are two objects with the same vertex numbering in which one has the vertices shaped specifically to represent some other pose or state of the mesh. The Blend Shape creates an offset value between the original object and the "target" object, transitioning between one and the other in a linear fashion. These blend shapes can then be mixed and matched with a series of sliders in the Blend Shape Editor.

In Figure 9.30 you can see the original deformation of the bicep in our skinned mesh. In order to create a corrective blend shape, duplicate the geometry and move it to the side. Next, you will sculpt the desired area manually using the vertex transform tools. Editing them based on the normal or normal average is a good way to gently sculpt certain areas in order to fix the deformation in the intended pose, in this case when the elbow is flexed 90°. Figure 9.31 illustrates the result of the vertex tweaking.

Once we have duplicated our original mesh, or base target, in the desired pose and sculpted the resulting area of the geometry, we will then need to generate a *corrective* blend out of the sculpted blend. There are several scripts out there that automatically calculate this offset. I use BSpiritCorrectiveShapes.mel, which you can find with the supplemental materials for this lesson on the publisher's website. Once you have sourced

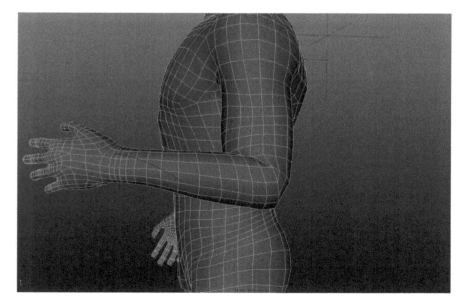

FIGURE 9.30 The original arm deformation. Not bad, but we can do better!

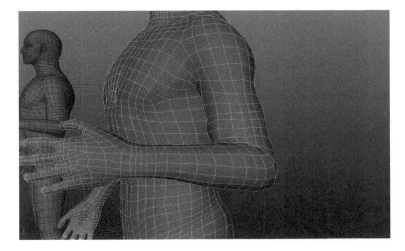

FIGURE 9.31   The sculpted blend shape for the elbow bend at −75°. We create our sculpt blend shapes in order to create the exact look we want at certain joint poses.

the script by dropping it in your user/maya/settings/ script directory, you can load it into the MEL script editor and run "BSpiritCorrectiveShapes" in the command line, which will execute it.

First, select the sculpted blend shape, and then select the base mesh. Type "BSpiritCorrectiveShapes" from the script editor. You should see a progress bar appear and calculate the offset of the vertices. Once it has completed, it will create a corrective version of the sculpted blend shape as a separate object, which you can see in Figure 9.32.

Now that we have a corrective shape to use as a target, let's create the Blend Shape Node! Select the corrective target first, and then add-select the base (skinned) mesh. Now you can open the Create Deformer > Blend Shape with the option box, as you see in Figures 9.33 and 9.34. Make sure that you name this node "Correctives," and choose "Front of Chain" from the drop-down menu in the second tab, as you can see in Figure 9.35. This sets the Blend Shape node in front of the other deformers, which is necessary to preserve the offsets of the skin cluster on top of the deformer stack.

We're almost home! Now we just have to *drive* the blend target value from 0 to 1, based on the rotation of the elbow from 0 to −75°. There are several different ways to do this—we can use an expression that would look like this: *Correctives.elbow75 = elbow.rotateX/-75*. That would "normalize" the rotation of the elbow from 0 to −75°, making a linear relationship between its value and the value of the corrective shape, like you can see in Figures 9.36 and 9.37.

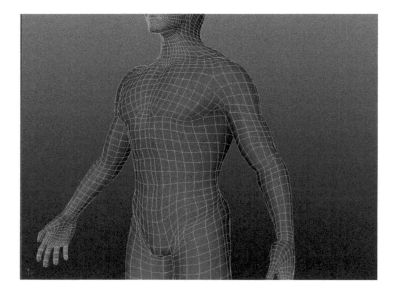

FIGURE 9.32 The corrective blend shape for the elbow bend at −75°. This is the actual target we'll use in the blend shape node, which will happen before the skin in the deformer stack. The vertices are in strange places, but that's because we have to add the offsets of the skin cluster on top of it.

Create Deformers	Edit Deformers
Blend Shape	□
Lattice	□
Wrap	□
ShrinkWrap	□
Cluster	□
Soft Modification	□
Nonlinear	▶
Sculpt Deformer	□
Texture Deformer	□
Jiggle Deformer	□
Jiggle Disk Cache	□
Jiggle Disk Cache Attributes	
Wire Tool	□
Wire Dropoff Locator	□
Wrinkle Tool	□
Point On Curve	□

FIGURE 9.33 With the corrective blend target and the base shape selected, open up the Create Blend Shape box.

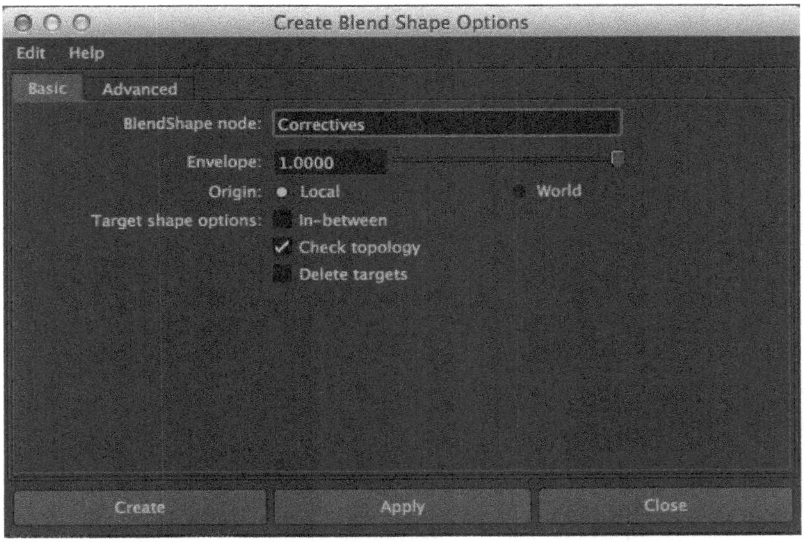

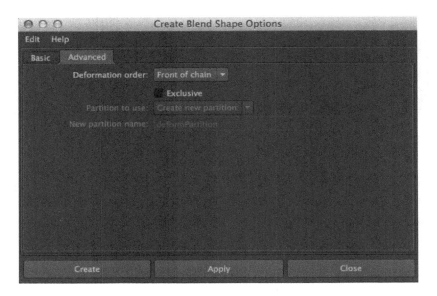

FIGURE 9.34   The options for creating a corrective blend shape.

FIGURE 9.35   Make sure that Front of Chain is selected! Without that the blend shape will override the skin cluster.

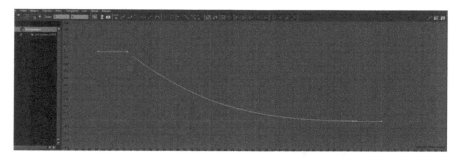

FIGURE 9.36   Expression to drive the blend shape channel.

FIGURE 9.37   The blend shape–driven key relationship in the graph editor.

We can also use a Driven Key to create the relationship between the two values. If you're using only Maya, this is the better way to go because you can choose the acceleration of the value change as well! In Figure 9.37, you can see how I ramp up the corrective blend shift as the elbow reaches its target of −75°, which allows me to fine-tune how the deformation occurs.

Using this simple procedure, you can create extremely sculpted characters with a much higher level of deformation than just skin weights alone. Sculpting, generating, and managing the Blend Shapes is a tough task, but once you are done the results will look great.

9.12 LESSON 5: THE TWIST RIG

I've saved the best for last! Well, maybe not the *best*, but at least the *hardest*. The twist rig is one of the most complex parts of a character rig, so I thought I'd wait until everything else was done.

As we discussed previously, a human arm is a complex mechanism. The action of the Humerus, Clavicle, and scapula is a machine with a lot of moving parts. Even though we aren't responsible for making it *exactly* like it is in real life, we're definitely responsible for making it *look* like it does in real life. One of the more difficult areas to conquer this is in the twisting aspect of the arm, which allows it a huge range of poses and flexibility. This twisting action comes from both the ball-in-socket joint of the Humerus *and* the ulna/radius combination in the forearm. If you want to see how much of each happens, use a marker to make two dots, one on your forearm and one on your bicep. Then roll your arm into various positions and see where those dots are pointing. You will see the two "planes" that need to shift on the limb in order to align them properly.

Twisting the upper and lower arm takes a specially constructed rig, which is fairly advanced but once you get the hang of what needs to be done it's not terribly difficult to recreate. The upper arm is the most difficult, since the twist nodes required to create the effect are inside the IK chain, which means that the X, Y, and Z axes of the Humerus must be controlled by the IK and not subject to individual manipulation. But the problem is the spin axis rotation (the Y-axis in this case) of the Humerus—it creates a totally improper deformation! You can see in Figure 9.38 how rotating the Humerus of our standard, minimal skeleton will twist the entire shoulder segment, causing it to look painfully broken.

So how do we fix this? We need to extract the spin axis rotation from our Humerus somehow and apply it to twist joints, which are in between the Humerus and the elbow. But the problem is that we can't really do this on the arm we intend to set up with the IK chain—it will control all the rotations of the joints inside of it. So for this reason, among a few others, we need to have *two* skeletons for our character. Yes, that's right! One skeleton is not enough! We really need an *animation* skeleton and a *deformation* skeleton. This allows us to put all of our complex deformations and extra nodes on one skeleton and *drive* it with another, simpler one. This sounds complex, but in reality it solves a lot of our problems.

How do we do it? We already *have* our skeleton, with skin weights and everything. Do we really have to make a new one and re-skin, re-paint,

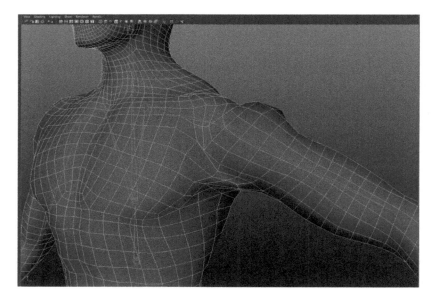

FIGURE 9.38   Ouch! The twisting of the Humerus on the spin axis is deforming our model in an incorrect manner.

and re-edit weights? The short answer is—yes. But we can make it slightly less painful. Simply duplicate the skeleton you already have, and prefix the hierarchy with ANI_, using the Modify > Prefix Hierarchy option in Maya (see Figure 9.39). This creates the animation skeleton and leaves the original in place, which is already deforming your model currently. Select the Hips Joint of the original skeleton and prefix the hierarchy name again, this time using DEF_. Now we have two skeletons! That wasn't so hard after all, was it?

Here's how the system works—we set up all of our animation controls and rigging on the animation skeleton—that way the animator works with controls that are as simple as possible. The animation skeleton also can take any standard motion capture data that uses this simple skeleton. The animation skeleton then controls the deformation skeleton, which contains all sorts of possible nodes to assist in getting the best deformation we can. Currently we are only interested in the twist nodes for the arm.

But we have to *drive* the deformation skeleton from the animation skeleton. There are a lot of ways to do this, but we want the fastest and most efficient method of making one skeleton move with the other. The most common method of doing this is with simple constraints. Currently we are only tinkering with the animation control of the arms, so we can create what are known as "pass-through" relationships between the joints in

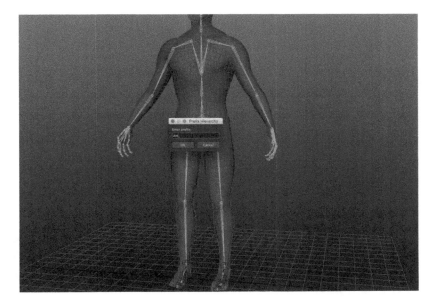

FIGURE 9.39 Prefix the hierarchy of the duplicate skeleton ANI_.

our deformation skeleton that just need their transforms to be exactly the same as the animation skeleton. The easiest way of doing this is to create a Parent Constraint between each ANI_ joint and each DEF_ joint in our skeleton. Select the ANI_Hips joint first, and then the DEF_Hips joint second. Open up the Constraint > Parent Constraint option box, and make sure that Maintain Offsets is off (Figure 9.40). This will ensure that the DEF_ joint in question moves with the ANI_ joint it is meant to follow. Do this for every joint in the skeleton EXCEPT for the arm joints, beginning with the Humerus and ending with the fingers.

Now we must create our twist joints. For a fully formed twist rig, we will need FOUR twist nodes in between the Humerus and elbow. You can use the Insert Joint Tool in Maya (Figure 9.41), which allows you to insert a joint between the beginning and end of a chain manually. I like to use the jgSplitJointChain.mel script, which you can easily find on Creative Crash and download for free (see Figure 9.42). This script will slice the joint chain into as many equal parts as you specify and parent them accordingly. Now we need to name them something appropriate. I use L_Humerus_Twist_25, L_Humerus_Twist_50, L_Humerus_Twist_75, and L_Humerus_Twist_100, so I know which joints are which. I am a stickler about naming joints for a reason! When your skeleton has 75 joints, you'll be really happy that you named them all exactly what they are.

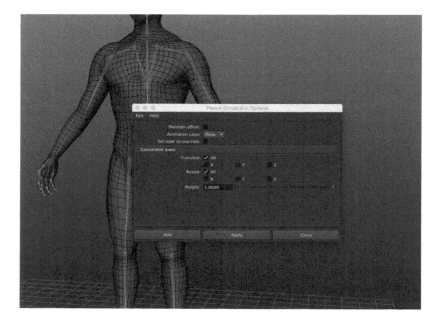

FIGURE 9.40   Parent Constrain the DEF_ joints to the ANI_ joints.

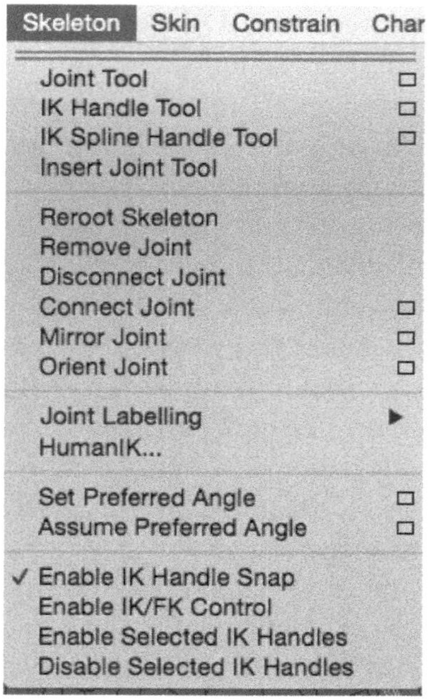

FIGURE 9.41   The Maya Insert Joint Tool.

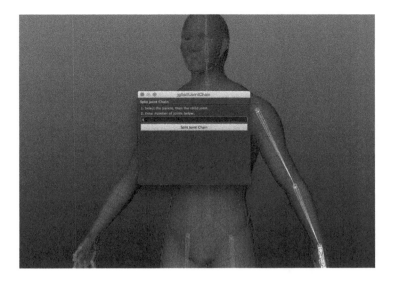

FIGURE 9.42   An easy-to-use joint splitting script, which is perfect for setting up twist rigs.

Now the fun begins! We need to add these joints to the influence list for our skin cluster and paint weights for them. In the real world, I always set this all up *before* I do skin weights, but this is as good a place as any to learn how to add influences for new joints.

This must be done for *every* joint, individually (yes, I know it's a pain, which is why I'd rather do it all at once). Select the joint you want to add and the bound skin you want to apply the changes to, and choose Skin > Add Influence from the drop-down menu (see Figures 9.43 and 9.44).

Now all you must do is paint the skin weights in the Artisan tools for every single one of the twist nodes, smoothing them out along the length of the arm in order to make the twisting action flow naturally, as you can see in Figure 9.45. When editing the skin weights, you will first have to "unlock" the weight value in the Paint Skin Weights Toolbox, as you can see in Figure 9.46.

We have a twist setup! What's next? Well now that we have the twist nodes added and weighted, we *must* figure out a way to pull the twisting action *off* of the animation Humerus (which is controlled by an IK setup) and *onto* the twist nodes, divided by a value of the number of twist nodes (four in this case). But we also need to make sure the DEF_Humerus follows the ANI_Humerus in everything except the spin axis (Y-axis in this case). How the heck do we do this?

FIGURE 9.43   Add Influence Action.

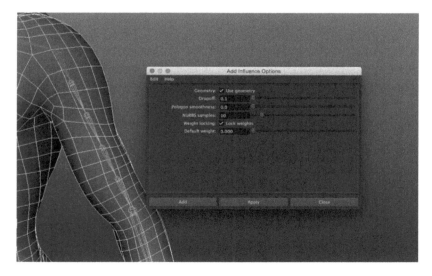

FIGURE 9.44   The Add Influence options. Make sure you lock weights with a value of zero! Otherwise your previous weighting will get ruined.

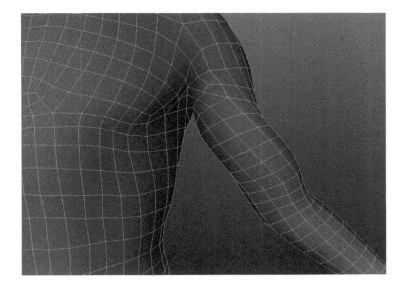

FIGURE 9.45   The nicely, smoothed, twist node weighting. It takes a while to do this right!

Elementary, dear Watson. Or at least, if it isn't elementary, we can figure something out… Basically what I want to do is to have the DEF_Humerus follow the ANI_Humerus, but only on the X- and Z-axis. If we use a Rotate-Plane IK solver with the Pole Vector at 0,0,0, we can essentially construct a system that will do this without much fuss. We can also create an Aim Constraint, but the IK solution here is way easier and more stable.

First we need to lock the rotation of the twist joints in all but the twist (Y-axis) to prevent them from rotating in unwanted ways by the Ik chain. You can turn off those degrees of freedom in the Attribute Editor, as seen in Figure 9.47.

Now we can create our Rotate Plane IK chain, from the DEF_Humerus to the DEF_Elbow. Once we have done this, select the IK handle that was created, naming it DEF_upperarm_IK_Handle (once again, so we know what it *is*), and look at the Channel Box. We want to change the Pole Vector channels to be 0,0,0. This keeps the IK chain from rotating on the spin axis completely! So as long as that IK handle moves with the ANI_Elbow, the DEF_Humerus will be in exactly the same rotation position but without the spin. All we need to do *now* is to create a Point Constraint from the ANI_Elbow (the target) to the DEF_upperarm_IK_ Handle. Since they're at the same place, there should be no need to maintain offsets (Figure 9.48).

FIGURE 9.46 **(See color insert.)** Make sure that the lock toggle button is in the off state for the newly added joints.

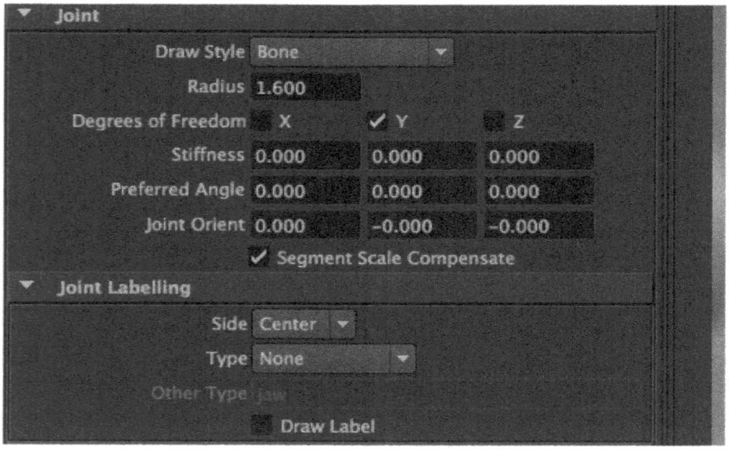

FIGURE 9.47 Turn off the degrees of freedom in the X- and Z-axis for the twist nodes in the upper arm.

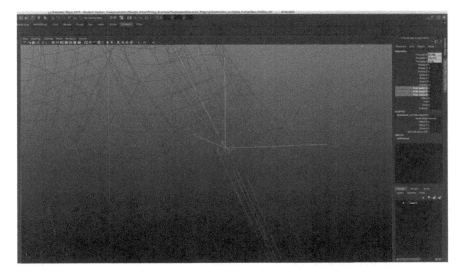

FIGURE 9.48 The DEF_upperarm_IK_Handle, which has been Point Constrained to the ANI_Elbow. All the Pole Vector values have been set to 0. This allows the DEF_Humerus to follow the ANI_Humerus, but without the twist!

Now that the DEF_Humerus can follow the ANI_Humerus without the twist, we will need to make the arm twist through the twist nodes, each of them twisting 25% of the DEF_Humerus twist value. We can do this easily with a simple expression for each of the twist nodes, as you can see in Figure 9.49.

If everything is done correctly, you should get a nice twisting of the arm when the ANI_Humerus joint rotates on the Y-axis! Figure 9.50 illustrates the result.

It's almost over! All we need to do now is the forearm twist. The nice thing about the forearm twist is that it doesn't need all the fancy rigging that the upper arm does. Since the wrist is free to rotate on its own axis, all we have to do is to create a Parent Constraint from the ANI_Wrist to the DEF_Wrist, which will force the DEF_Wrist to follow the animation skeleton. Then we use the same expression as we did for the upper arm twist nodes, dividing the ANI_Wrist Y-axis rotation by 4 for each forearm twist joint. Of course, you'll have to create the twist nodes, insert them into the skin cluster, and then paint the weights for each one (which is so much fun to do). In the end, you should have a nice, smooth, twisting setup that will really enhance the deformation of your

FIGURE 9.49 This expression should be put on each of the twist nodes.

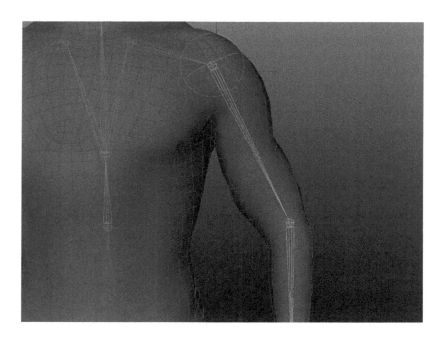

FIGURE 9.50 **(See color insert.)** It was a lot of work, but look at the end result! Much better than Figure 9.38!

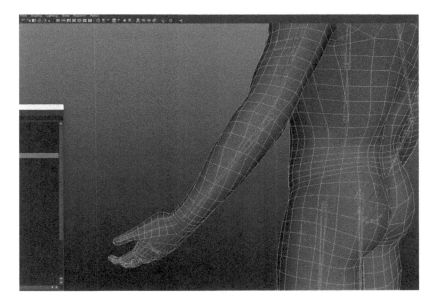

FIGURE 9.51   The twisting forearm.

character. I know that the twist nodes are a pain to create, bind, and skin, but a good deformation model is really important when rigging a full, flesh character. It's important to note that if the character is wearing a shirt of some kind, then the twist of the forearm and upper arm isn't visible, so you don't really *need* a twist setup. Always go for the path of least resistance (Figure 9.51).

CHAPTER 10

Conclusion

THIS BOOK HAS TAKEN you, the aspiring character rigger, through all the principles and applications you need to be able to set up a character rig of your own. One of the things I have to stress is the complexity of the material you are undertaking! There are multiple ways to set up a character, and this only gives you the *basic*, most commonly used tools in the industry. Hopefully you can extract the concepts and fundamental building blocks of knowledge from the lessons and information here to build your own rigs! I encourage the aspiring rigger to experiment with multiple techniques, and even work out your own solutions to various problems. There are so many things you can do that to list them all would be impossible. You must create the method of rigging based on your knowledge of the tools available and the constraints given.

I'd like to add a word here about the future of character rigging. Currently, there are multiple autorigging solutions that have built systems based on decades of rigging research and experimentation on the human body, how it moves, and how best to re-create that in a 3D setup. Autodesk's Human IK and Unity's Mecanim are two examples of this. Are these good? Are they bad? Does this mean nobody will have to rig characters anymore?

Those are all good questions, and just like the advent of using motion capture data for animation decades ago, there are some concerns about the *need* for the rigger. I think that rigging remains a necessary step in the development of character art for games and cinema, but the job of the rigger, much like the job of the animator, will eventually fundamentally change as the technology adapts and builds on itself. The autorigging solutions are only going to get better, but little details like skin weights, facial animation, and sculpted blend shapes are all part of the greater rigging pipeline. Using these autosolutions will simplify the tasks of the rigger and make his or her job more about *detail*, making the deformation as beautiful and natural as possible, which will end up giving us more and more realistic art.

Index